Marketing Precedes T

Calvin Grondahl

Signature Books
Salt Lake City, Utah

Nine of the ninety-four cartoons appearing in this compilation
previously appeared in the *Ogden Standard Examiner;*
three have previously appeared in *Sunstone* magazine.

Cover design by Smith and Clarkson

2003   2002   2001   2000   99   10   9   8   7   6

ISBN 0-941214-63-X

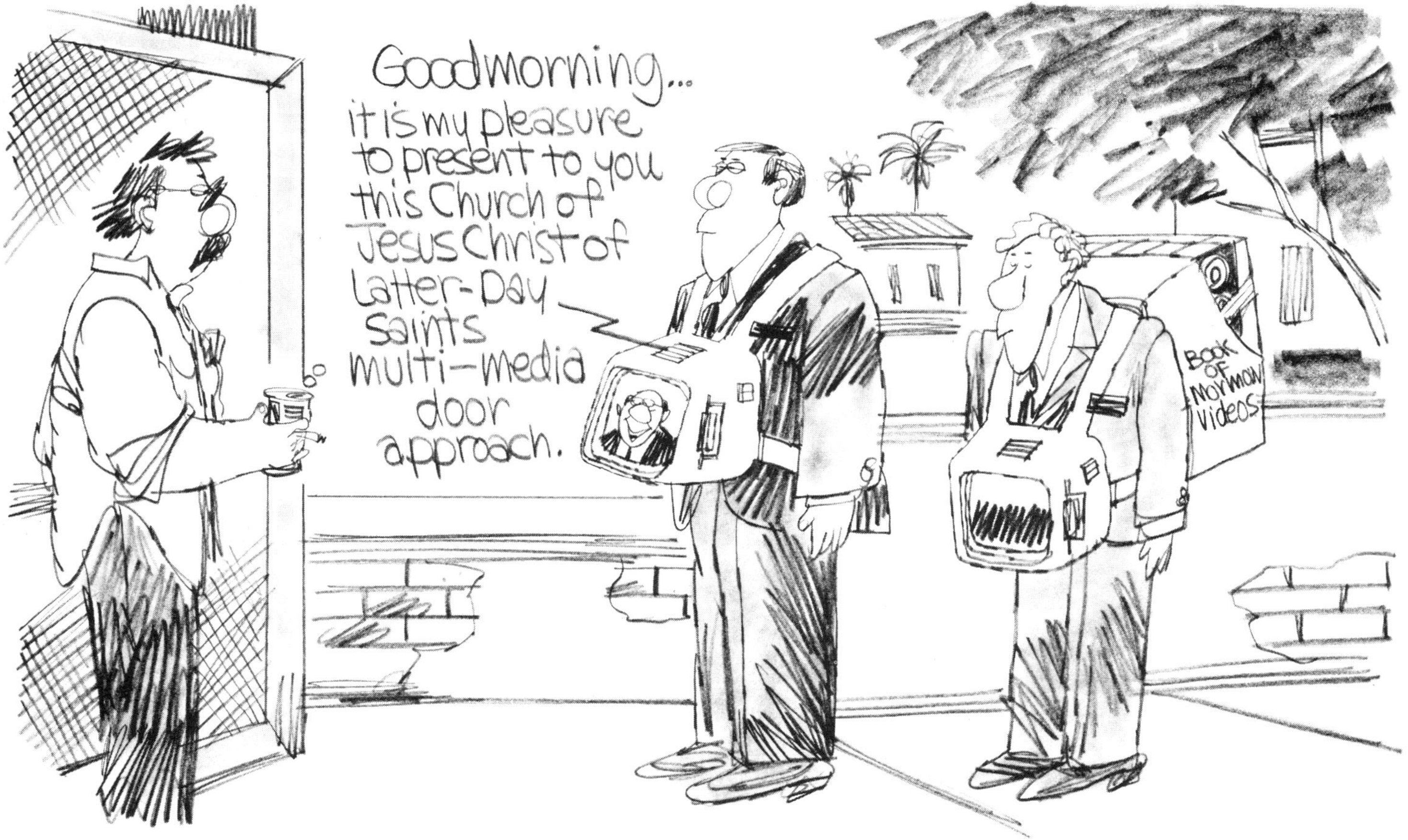
Goodmorning...
it is my pleasure to present to you this Church of Jesus Christ of Latter-Day Saints multi-media door approach.
Book of Mormon Videos

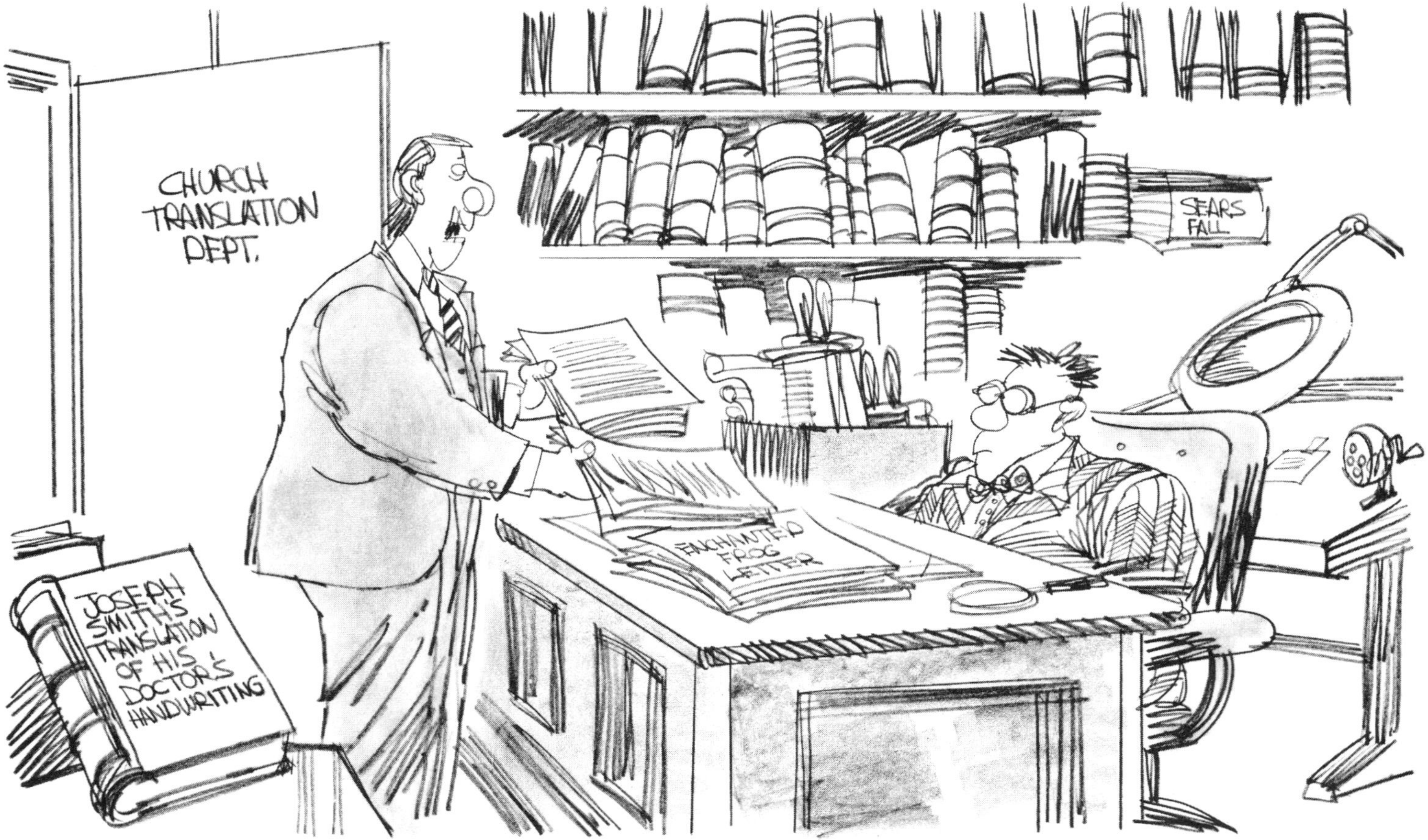
CHURCH
TRANSLATION
DEPT.
SEARS
FALL
JOSEPH
SMITH'S
TRANSLATION
OF HIS
DOCTOR'S
HANDWRITING
ENCHANTED
FROG
LETTER

"Is there any way we can translate these historical documents so they say 'folk dancing' instead of 'folk magic'?"

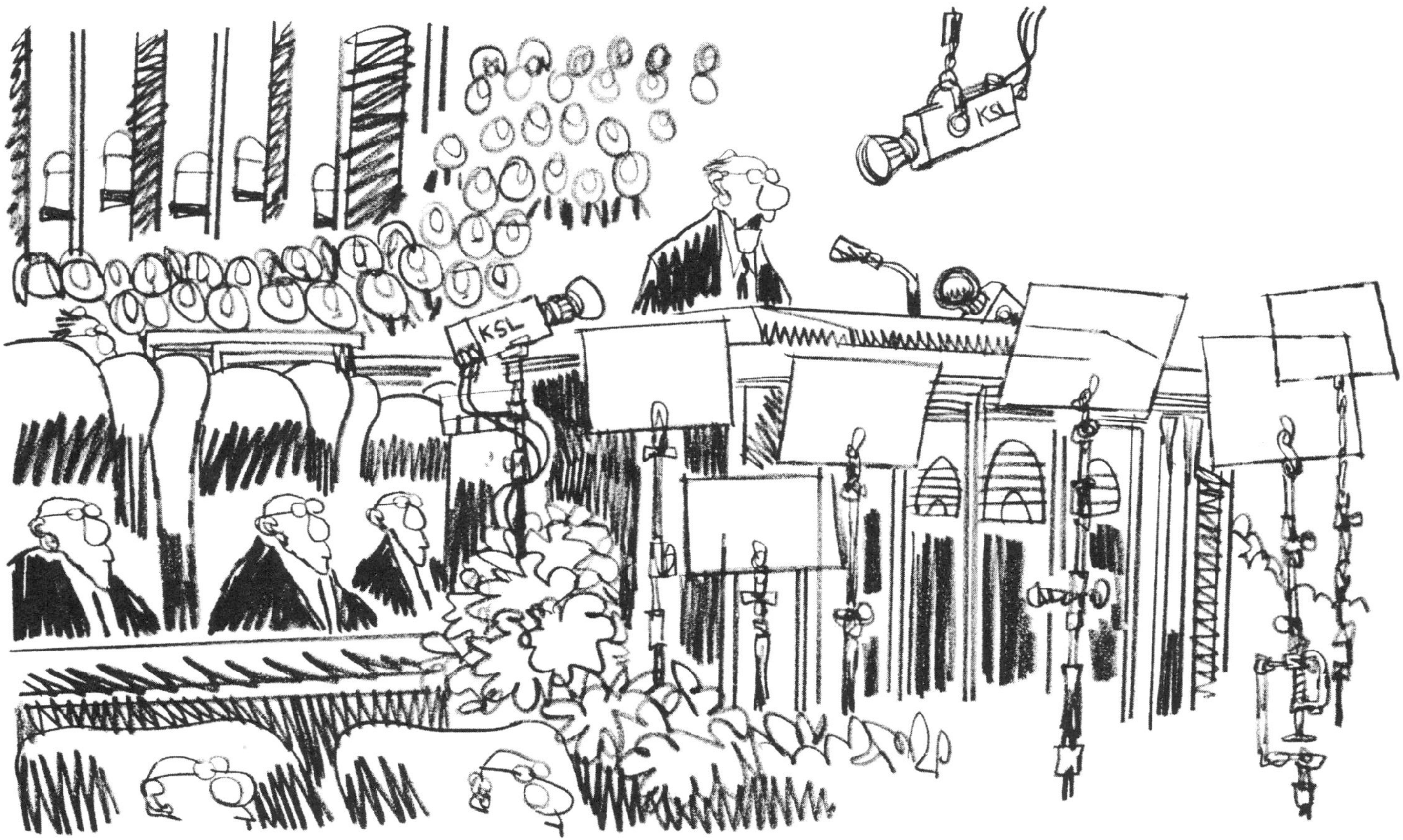
KSL
KSL

"Like Mormon of old, I shall make an abridgment of my words to fit them all in before the next station break."

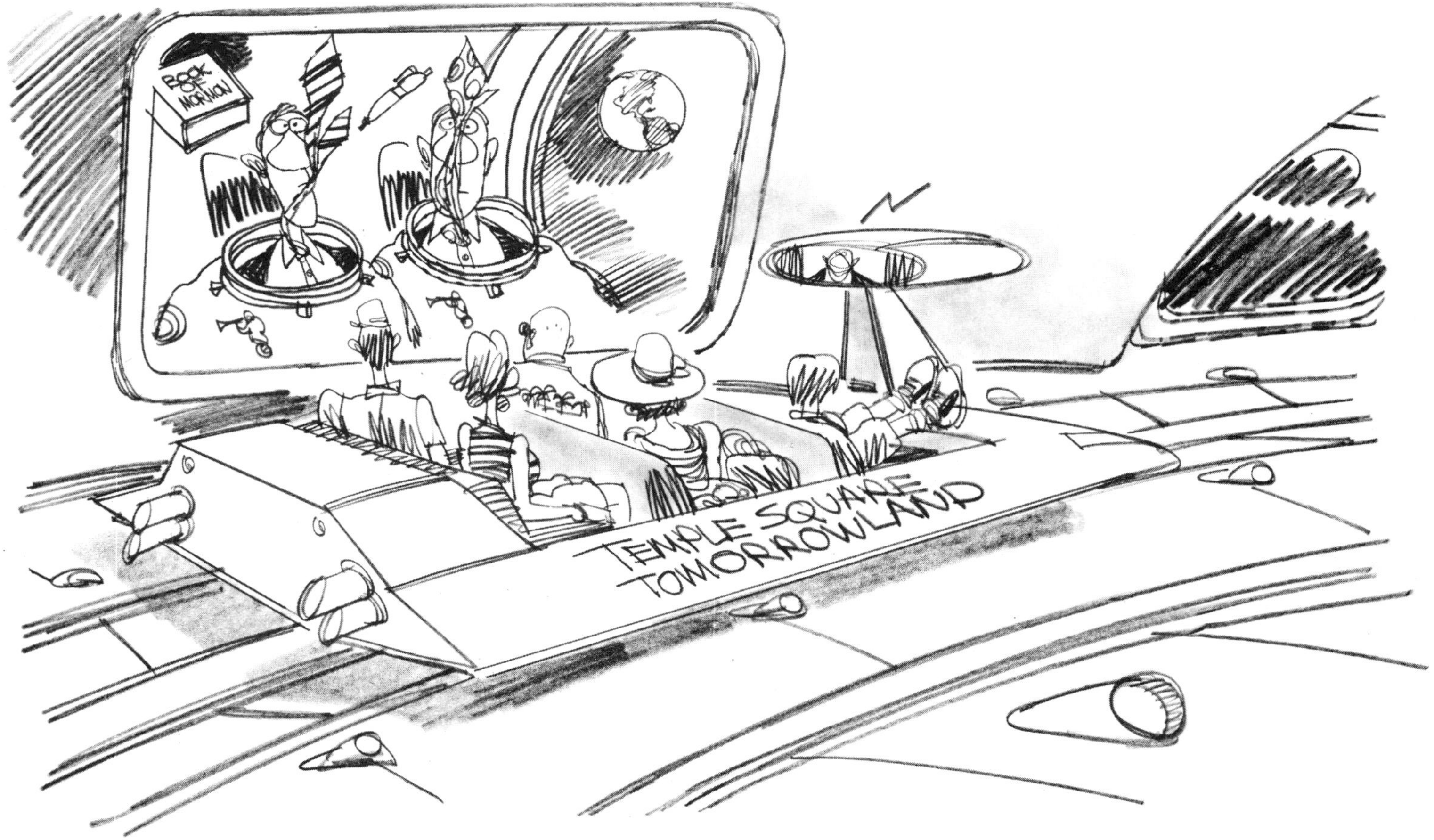
BOOK OF MORMON
TEMPLE SQUARE
TOMORROWLAND

"Missionaries in space will face difficulties never experienced before."

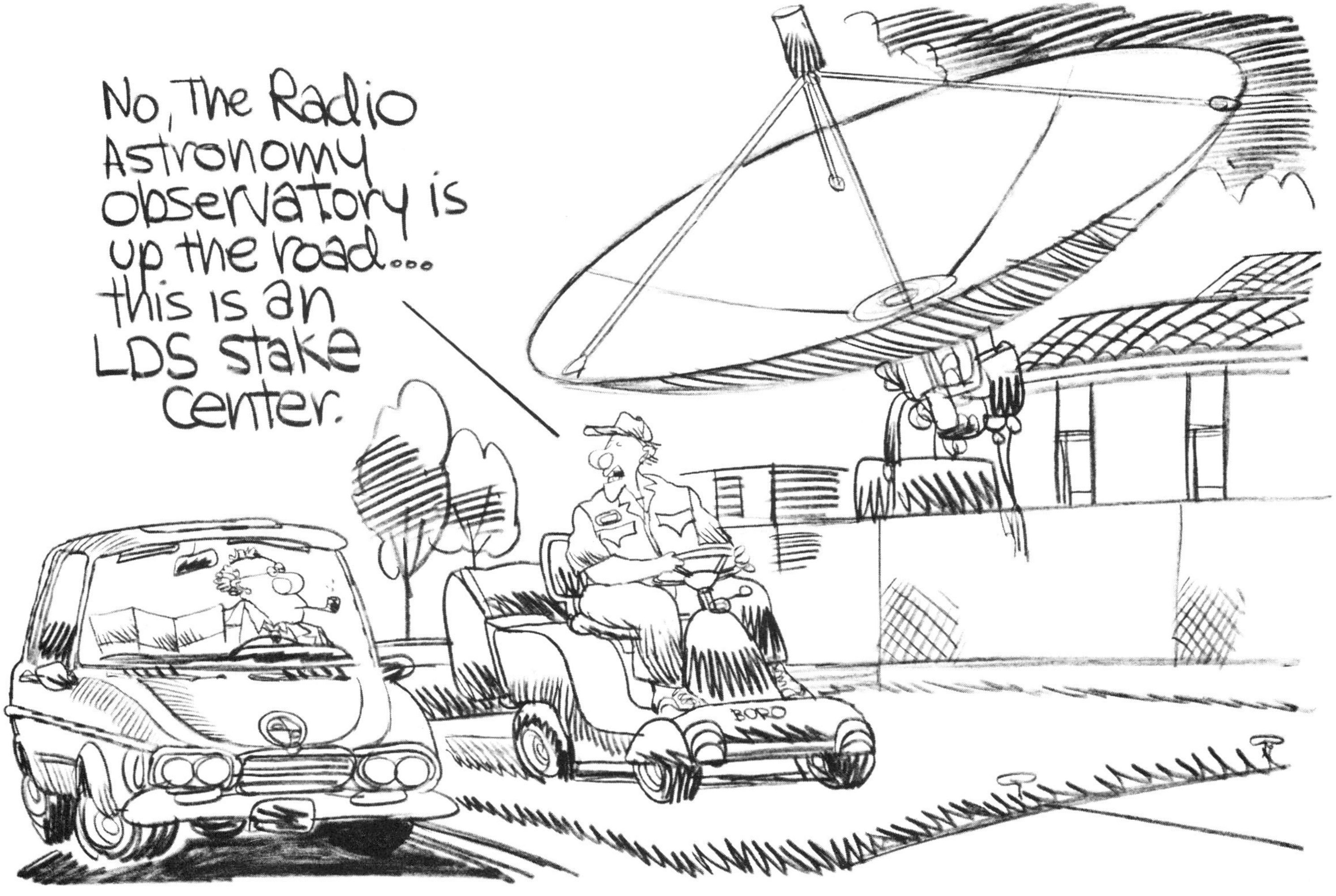
No, The Radio Astronomy observatory is up the road... this is an LDS stake center.
BORO

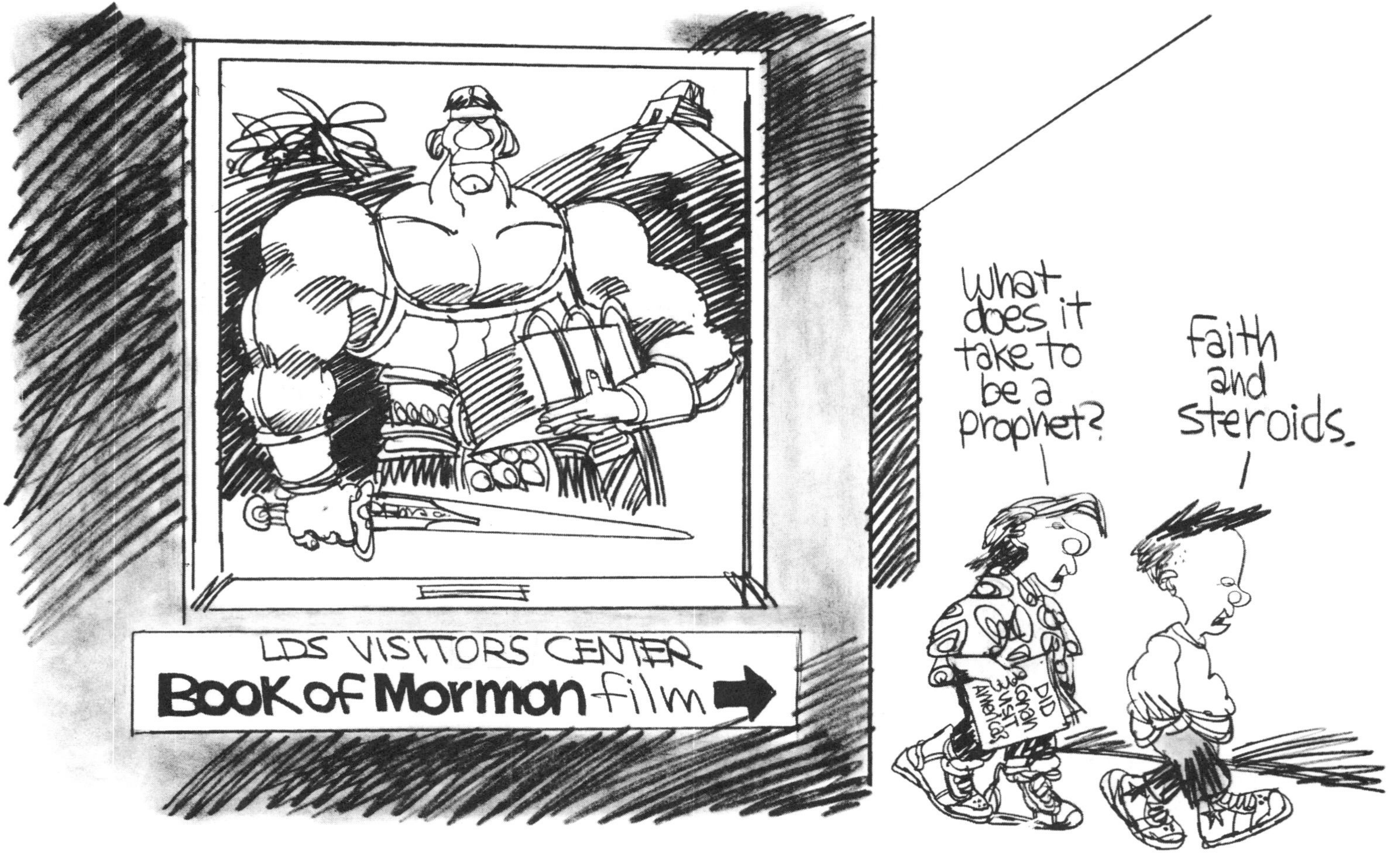
LDS VISITORS CENTER
Book of Mormon film
DID Conan VISIT America
What does it take to be a prophet?
Faith and steroids.

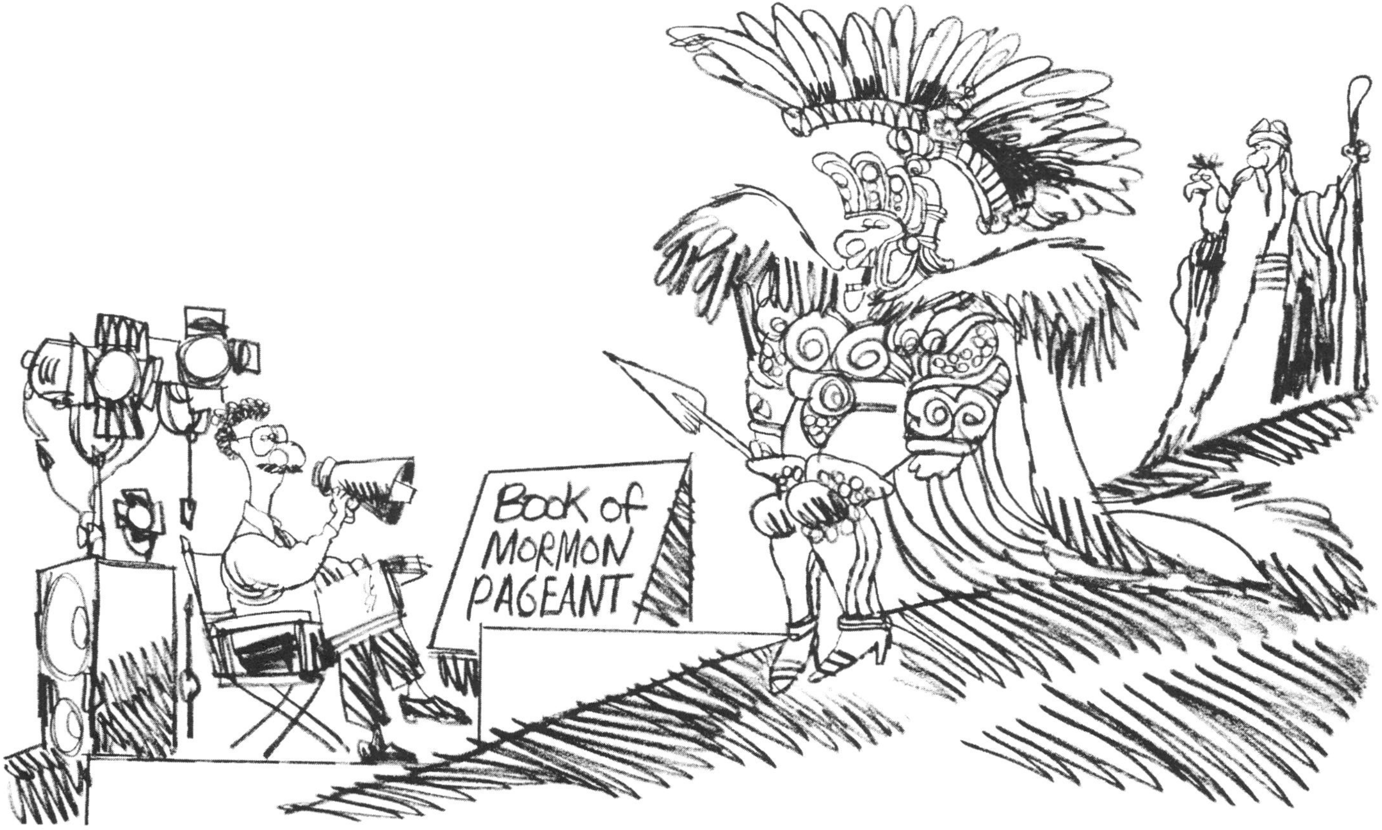
Book of
MORMON
PAGEANT

"I've got just one question. Did Captain Moroni really dress like a Las Vegas showgirl?"

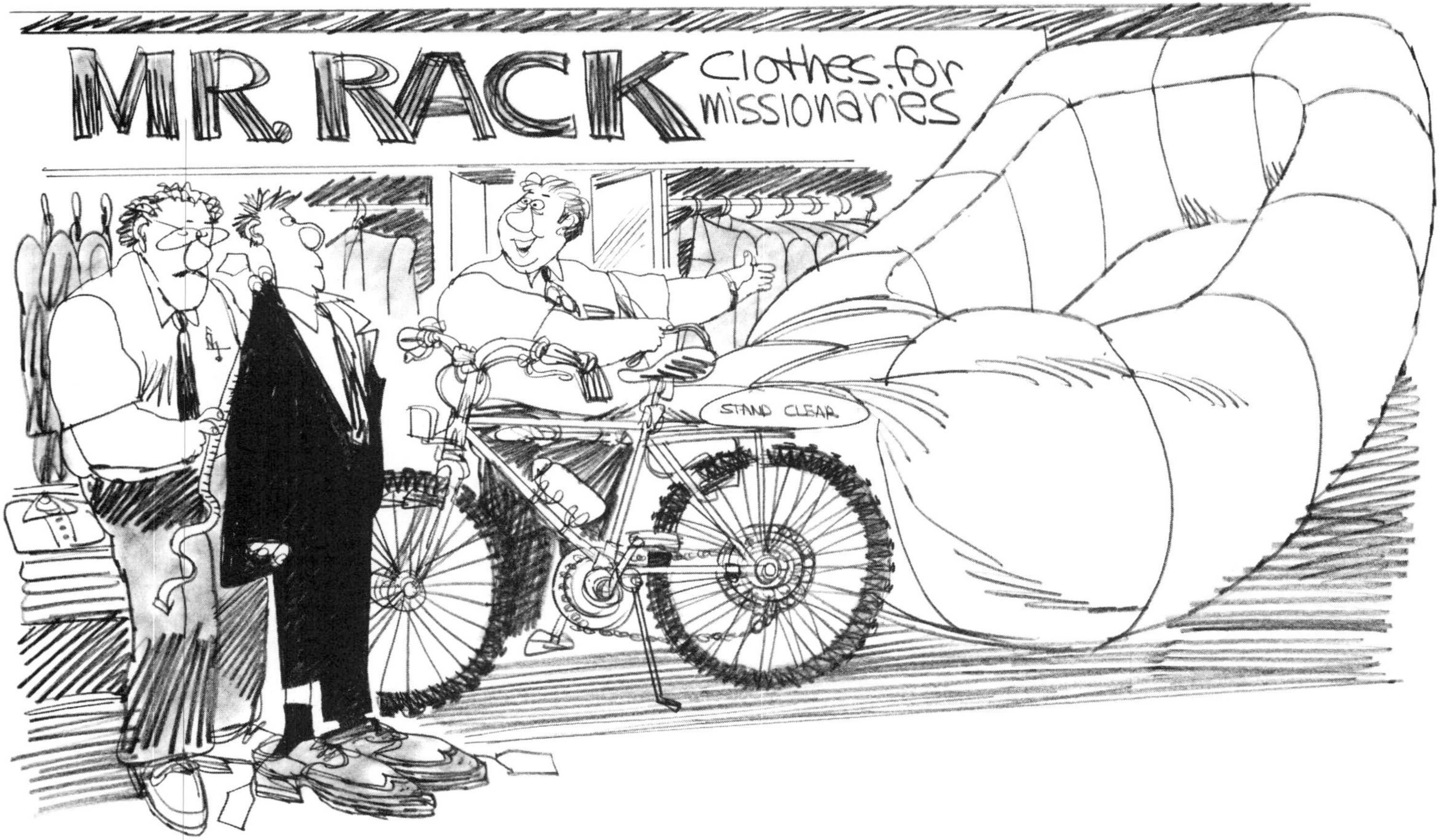
MR. RACK clothes for missionaries
STAND CLEAR

"It's an inflatable baptismal font. I'm surprised your mission hasn't asked you to bring one."

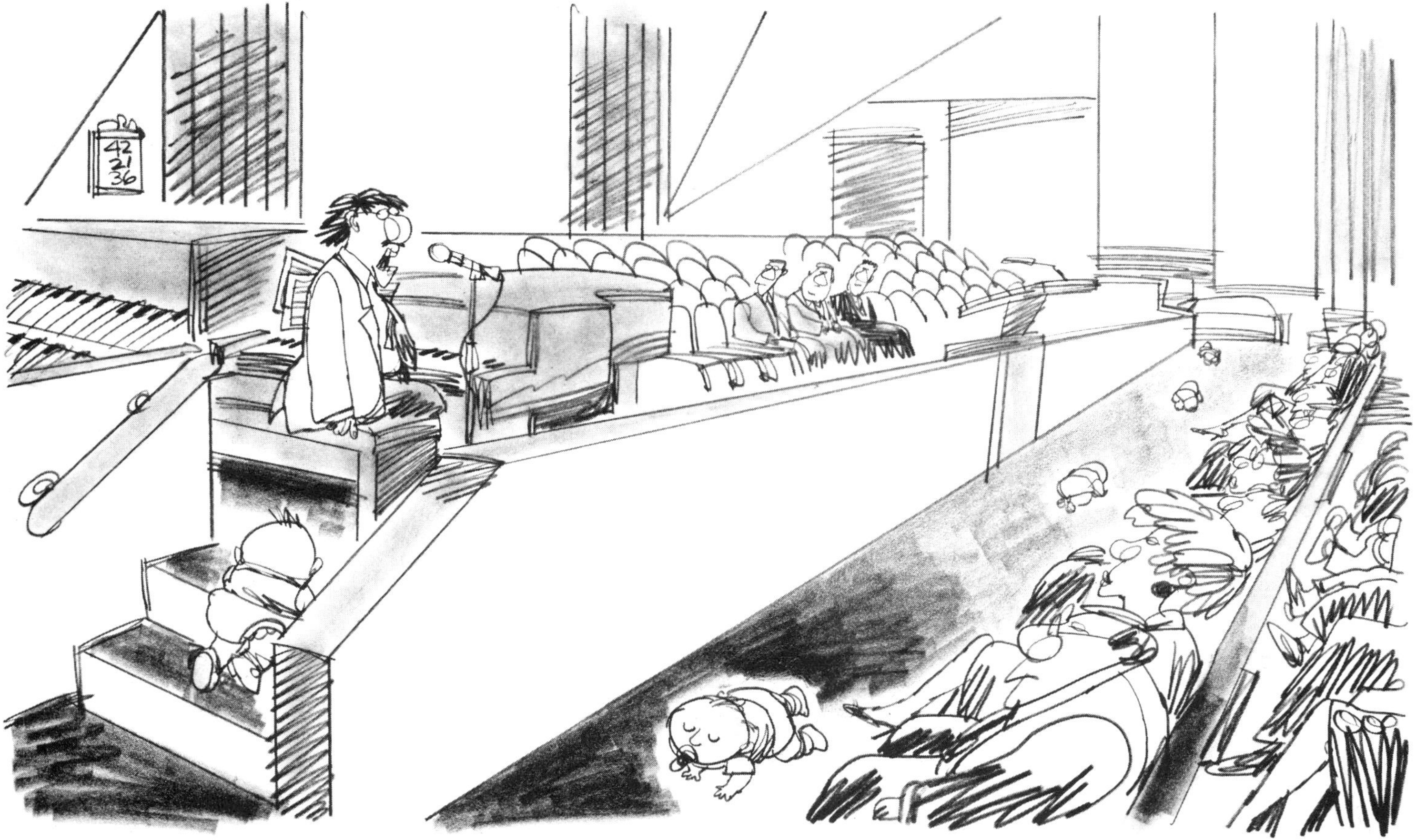
42
21
36

"I'd like to play this afternoon 'I Walked Today Where Mozart Walked.'"

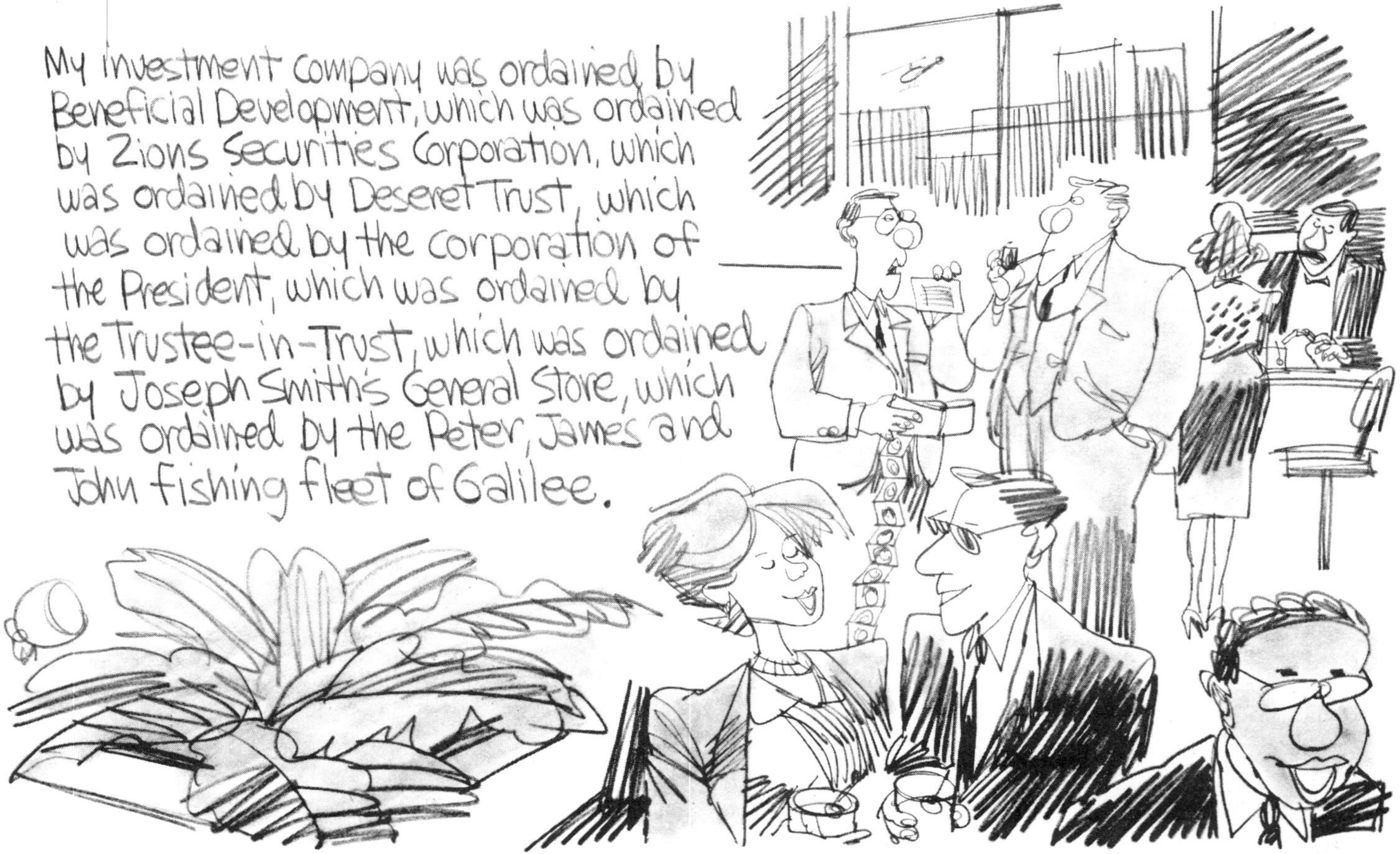
My investment company was ordained by Beneficial Development, which was ordained by Zions Securities Corporation, which was ordained by Deseret Trust, which was ordained by the corporation of the President, which was ordained by the Trustee-in-Trust, which was ordained by Joseph Smith's General Store, which was ordained by the Peter, James and John fishing fleet of Galilee.

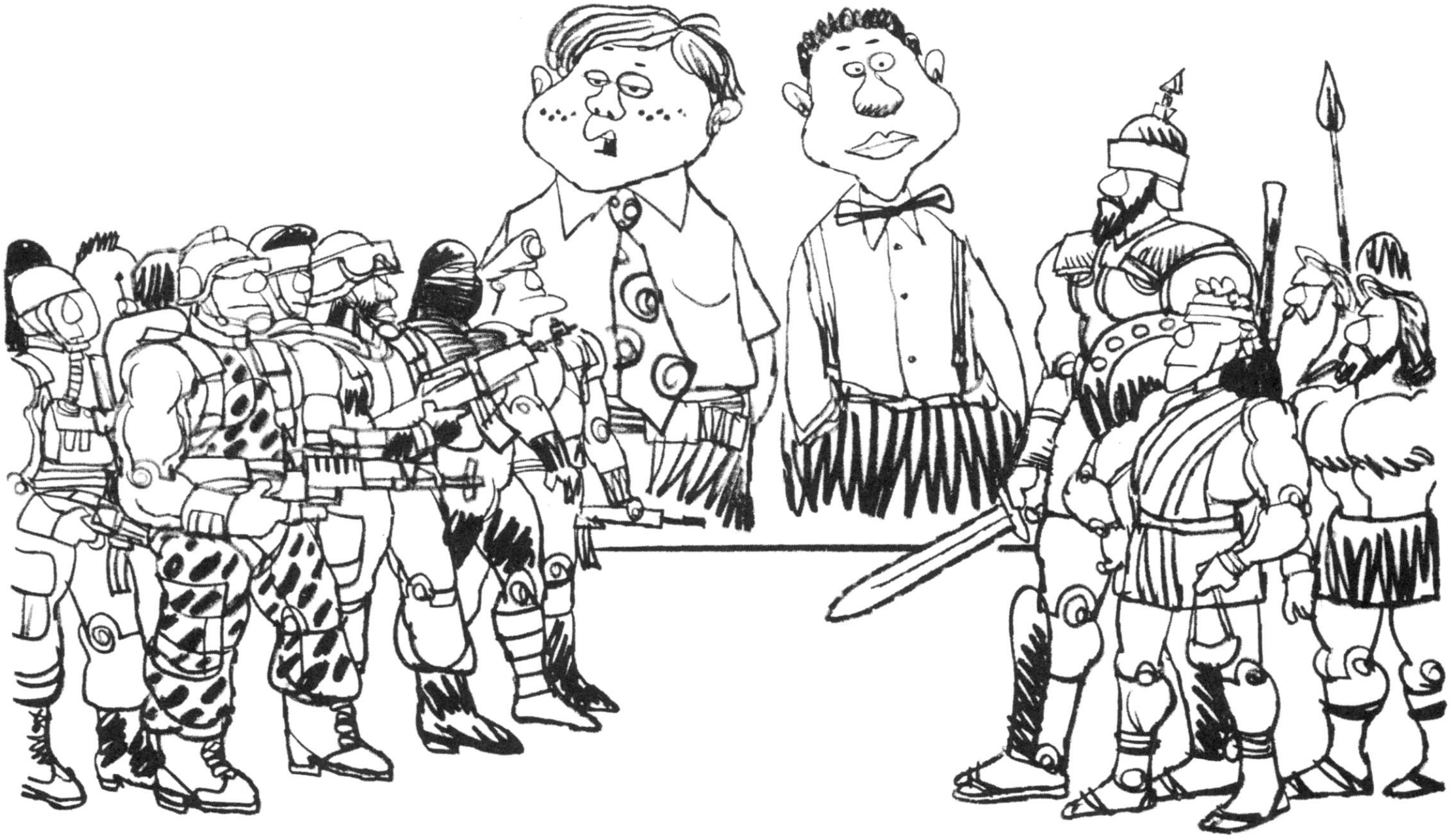

"Six days of the week it's G.I. Joe, Transformers, and Masters of the Universe. But on the seventh day it's Heroes of the Book of Mormon."

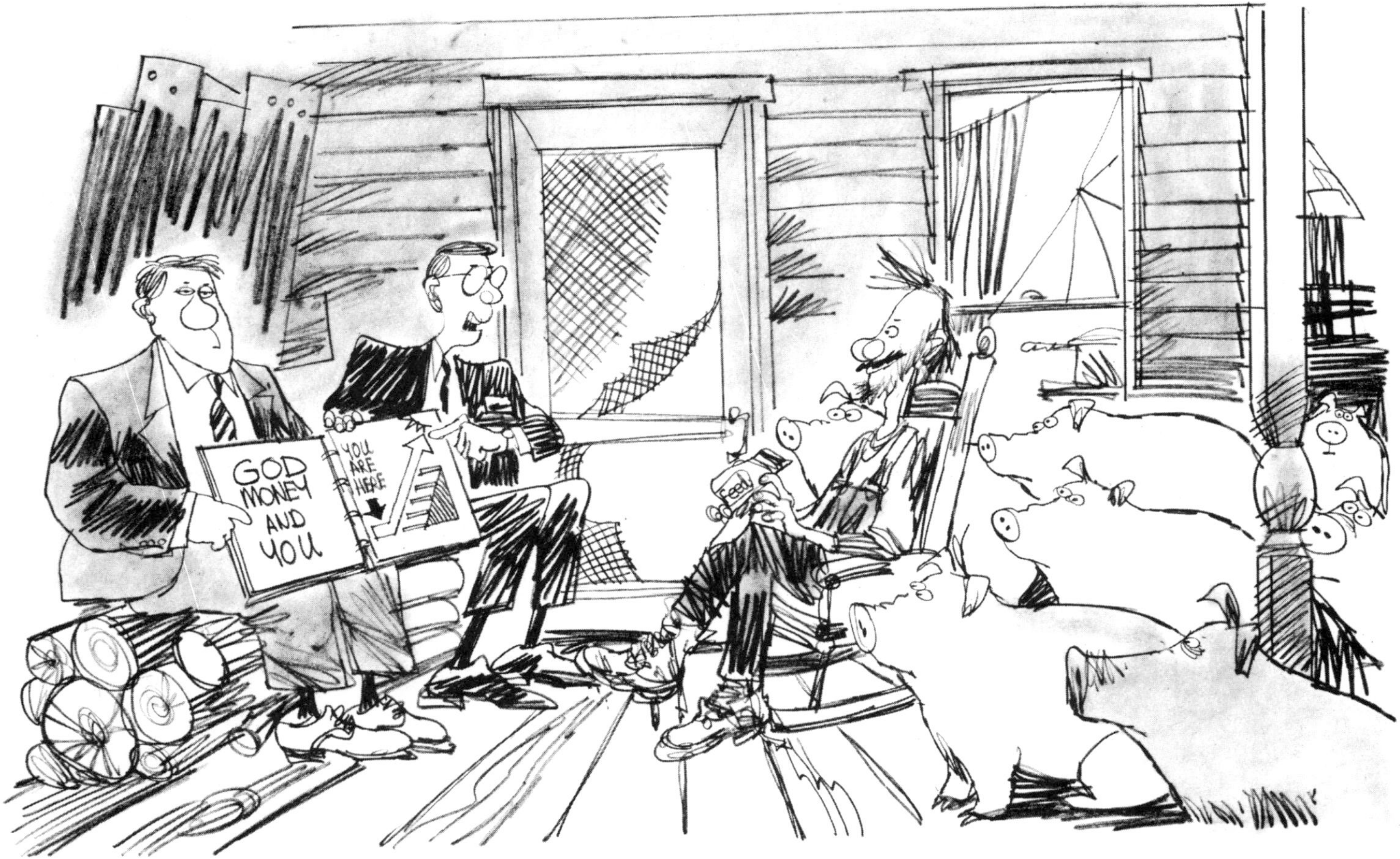
GOD MONEY AND YOU
YOU ARE HERE
Feed

"Faith. Repentence. Baptism. The gift of the Holy Ghost. Planning your life down to the second. And on to greatness."

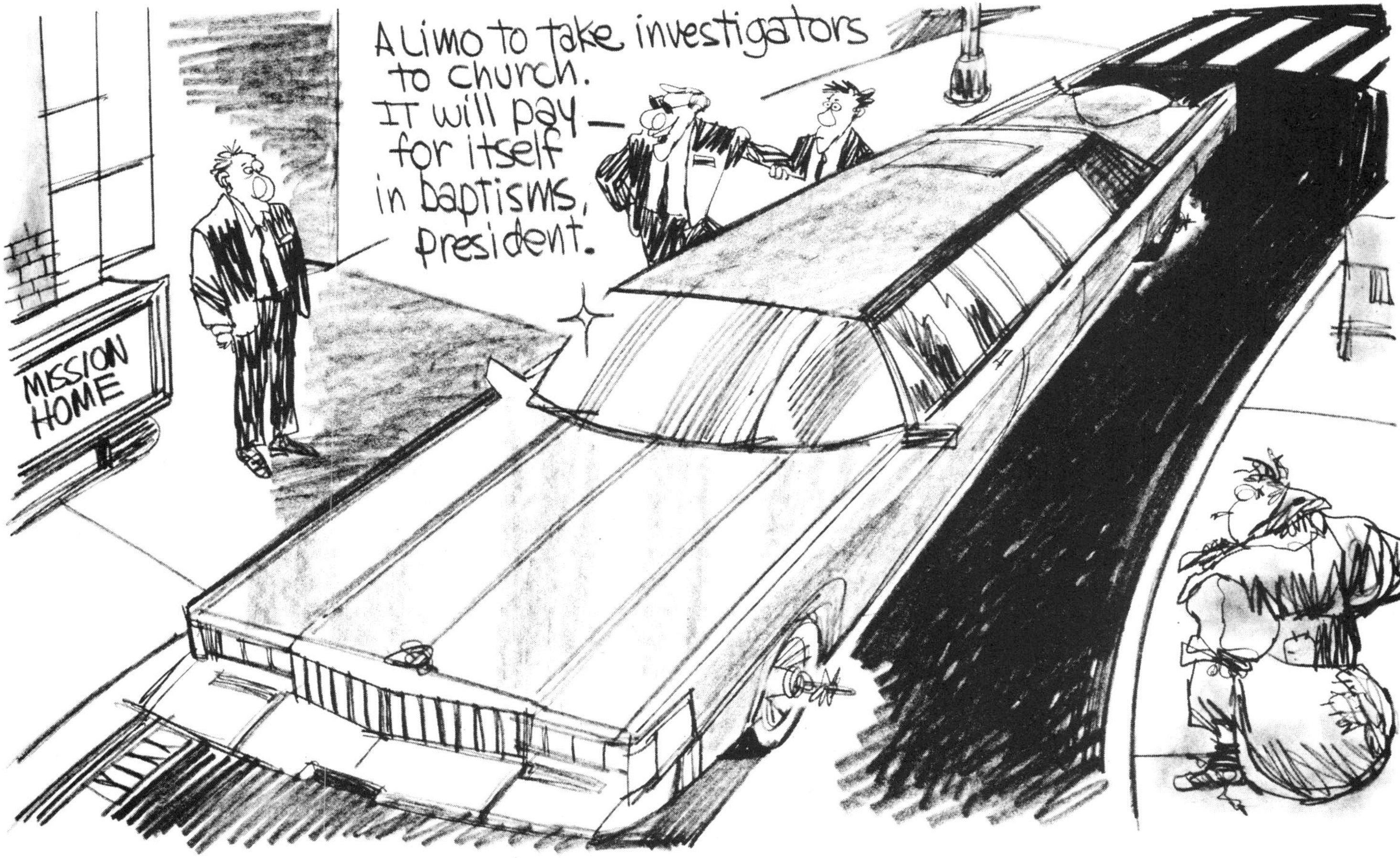
A Limo to take investigators to church. IT will pay — for itself in baptisms, president.
MISSION HOME

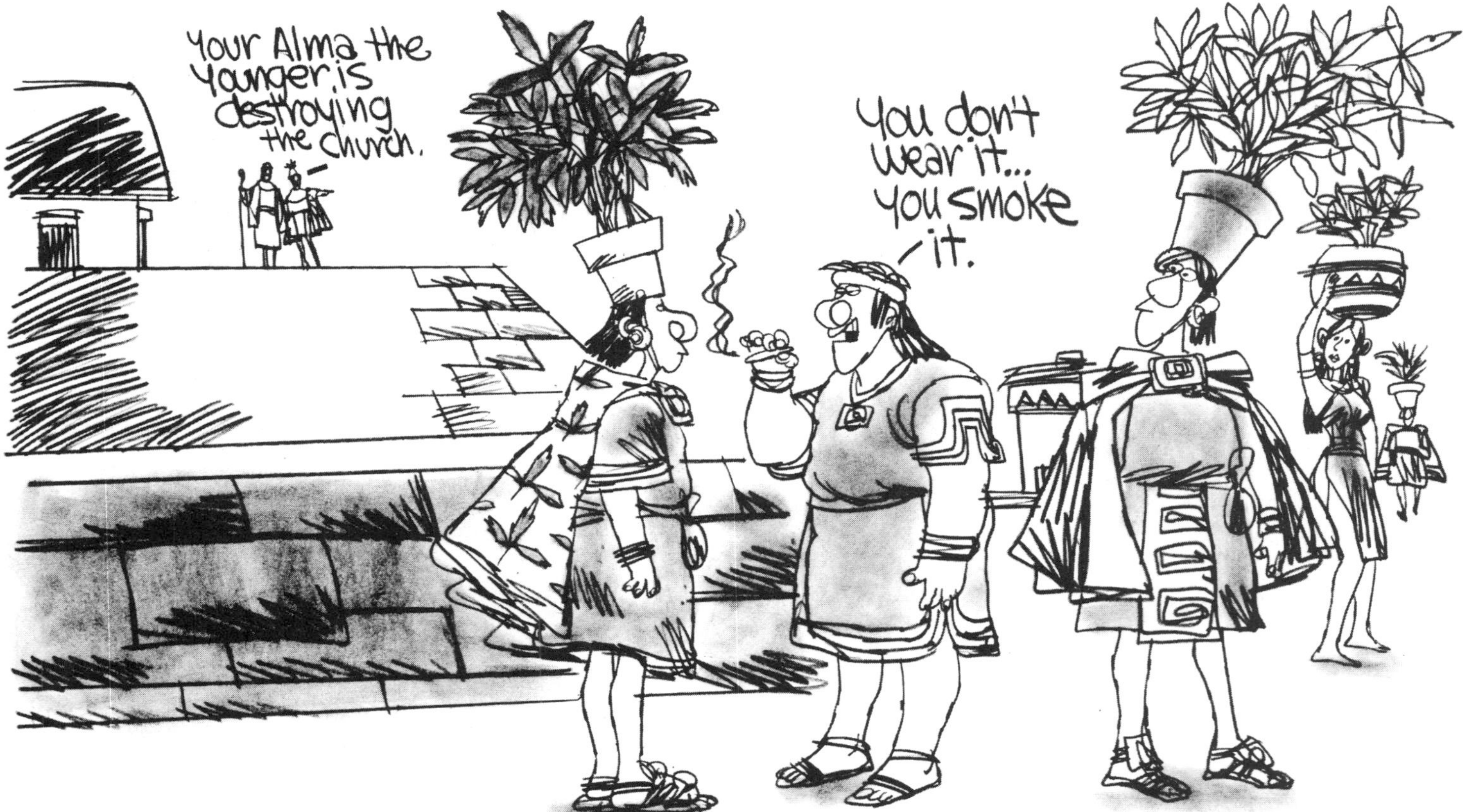
Your Alma the Younger is destroying the church.
You don't wear it... You smoke it.

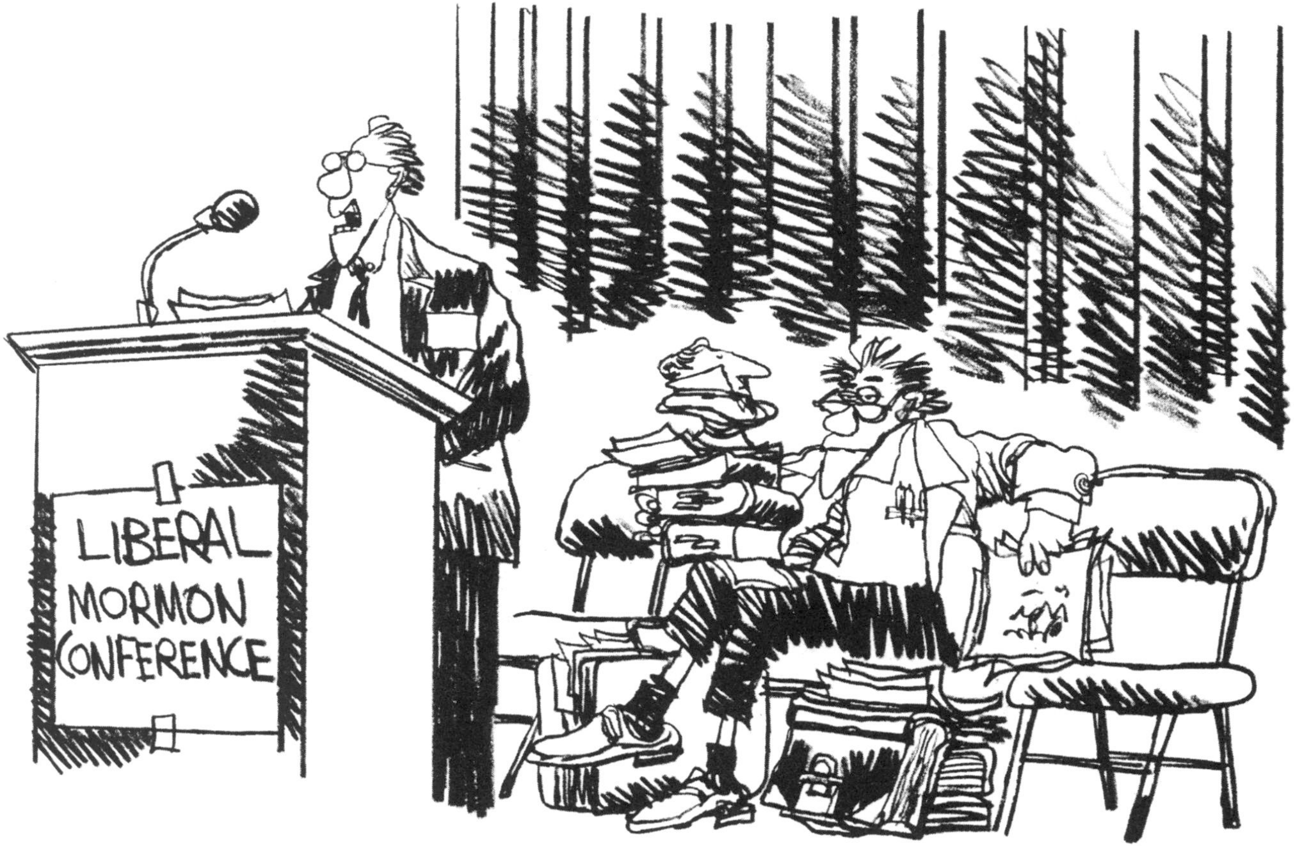
LIBERAL
MORMON
CONFERENCE

"At the age of six our next speaker wrote his first essay, 'Spiritual Equinox of the Paranormal Dimension,' but it was rejected by the *Children's Friend* as being too controversial."

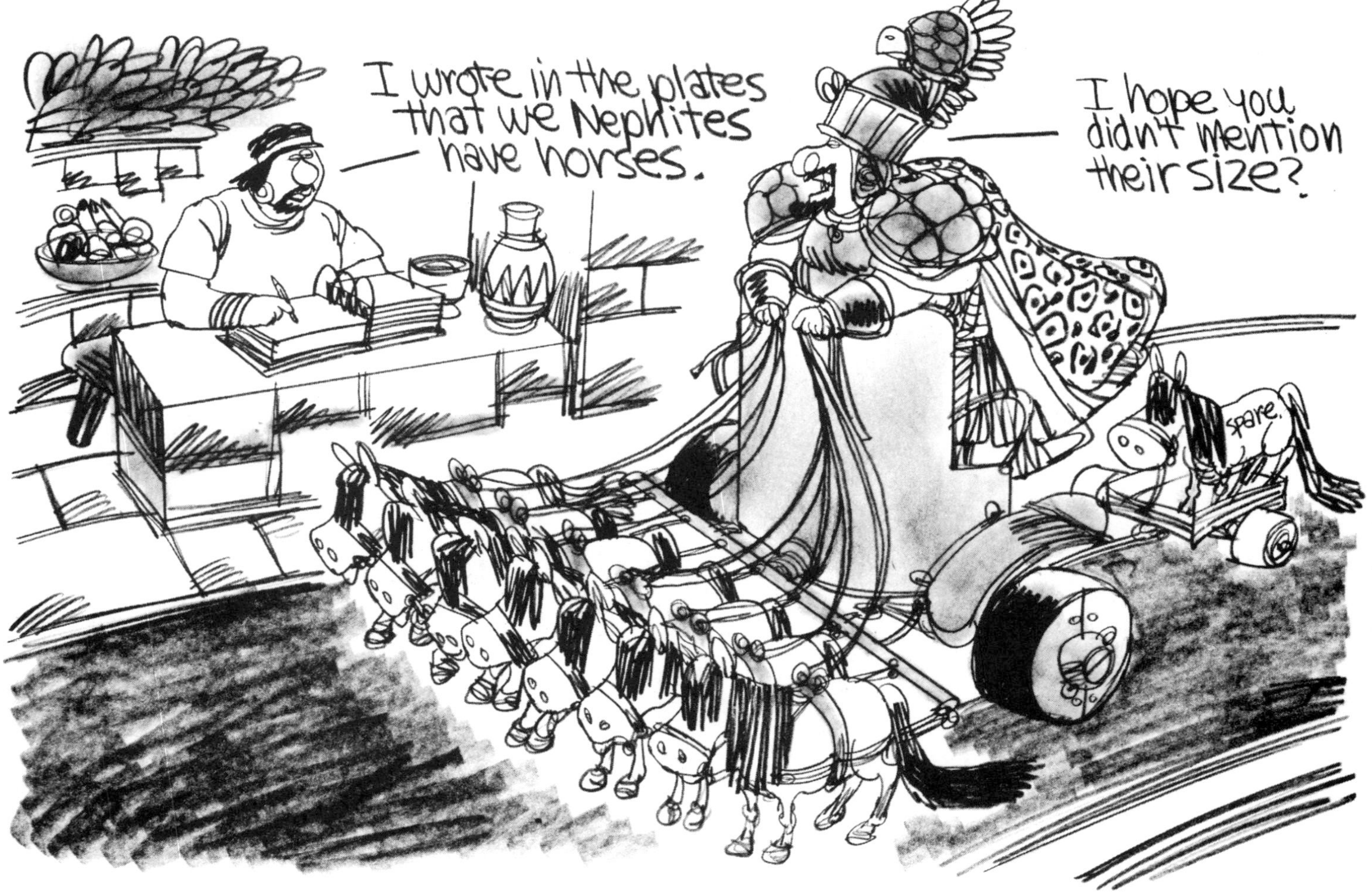
I wrote in the plates that we Nephites have horses.
I hope you didn't mention their size?
spare.

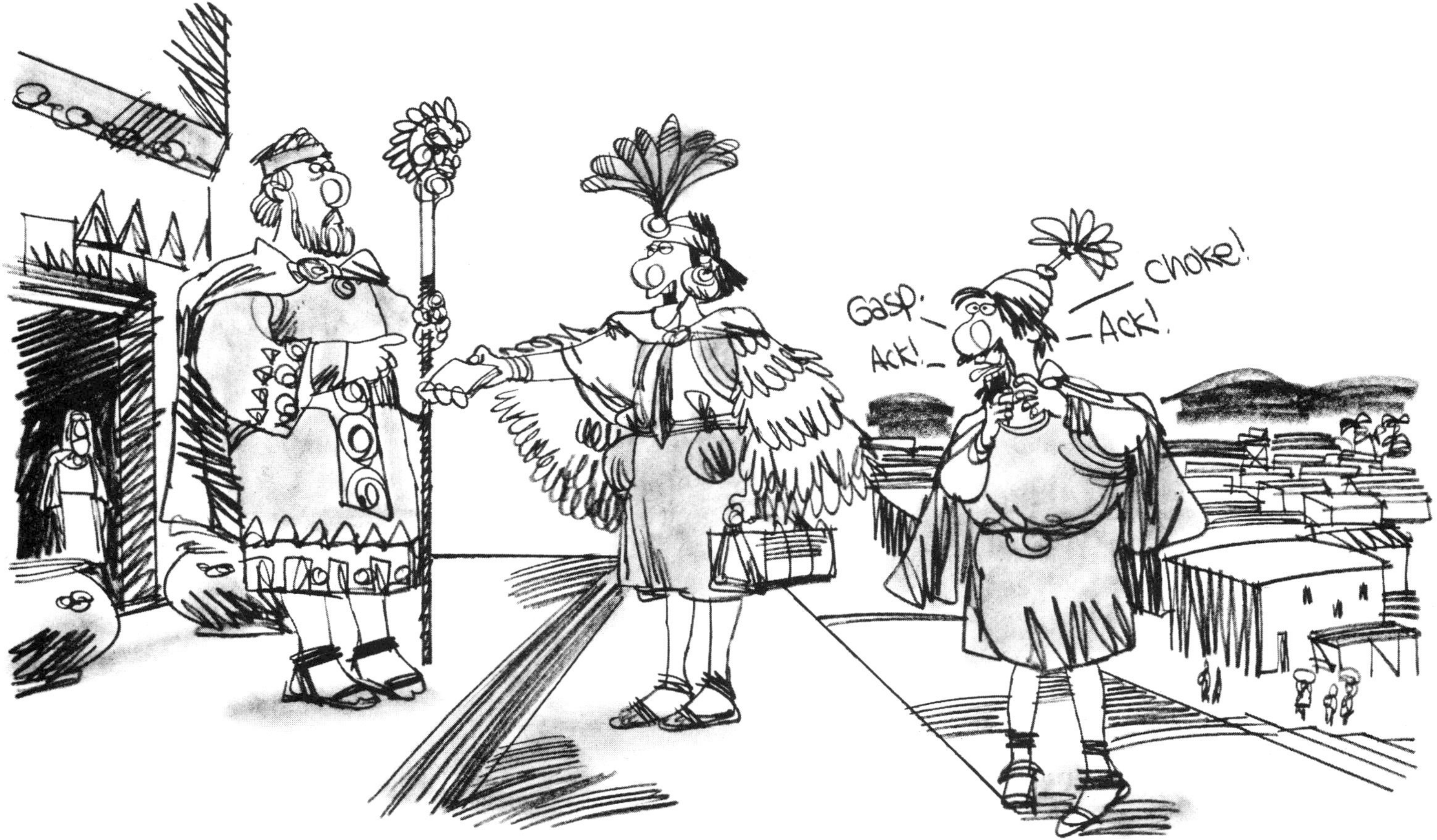
Gasp!
Ack!
Choke!
Ack!

"I represent the law firm of Zoke, Zim, Zor, and Zoe of Zarahemla. And we are filing suit against you on behalf of our client, Mr. Korihor."

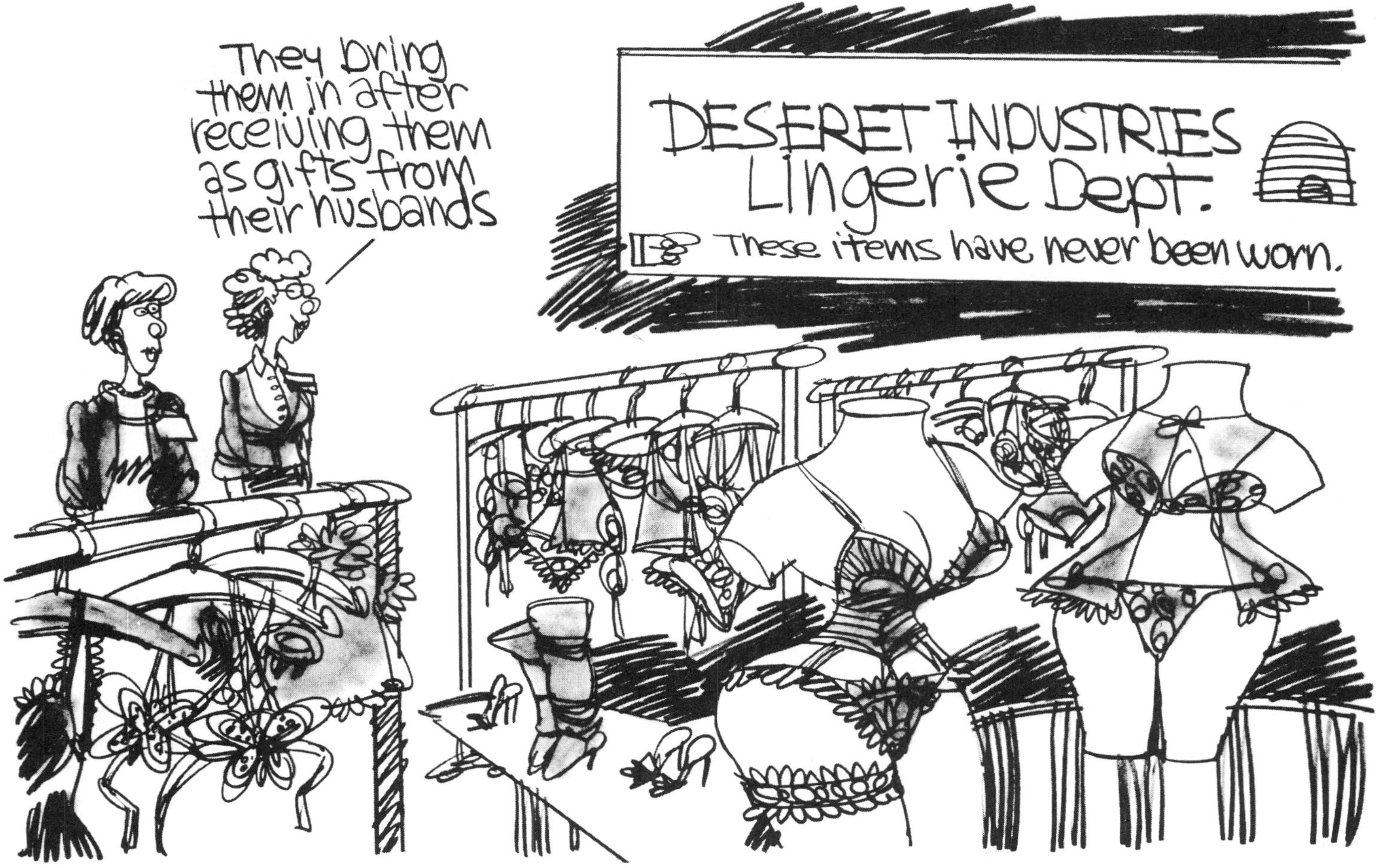
They bring them in after receiving them as gifts from their husbands
DESERET INDUSTRIES
Lingerie Dept.
These items have never been worn.

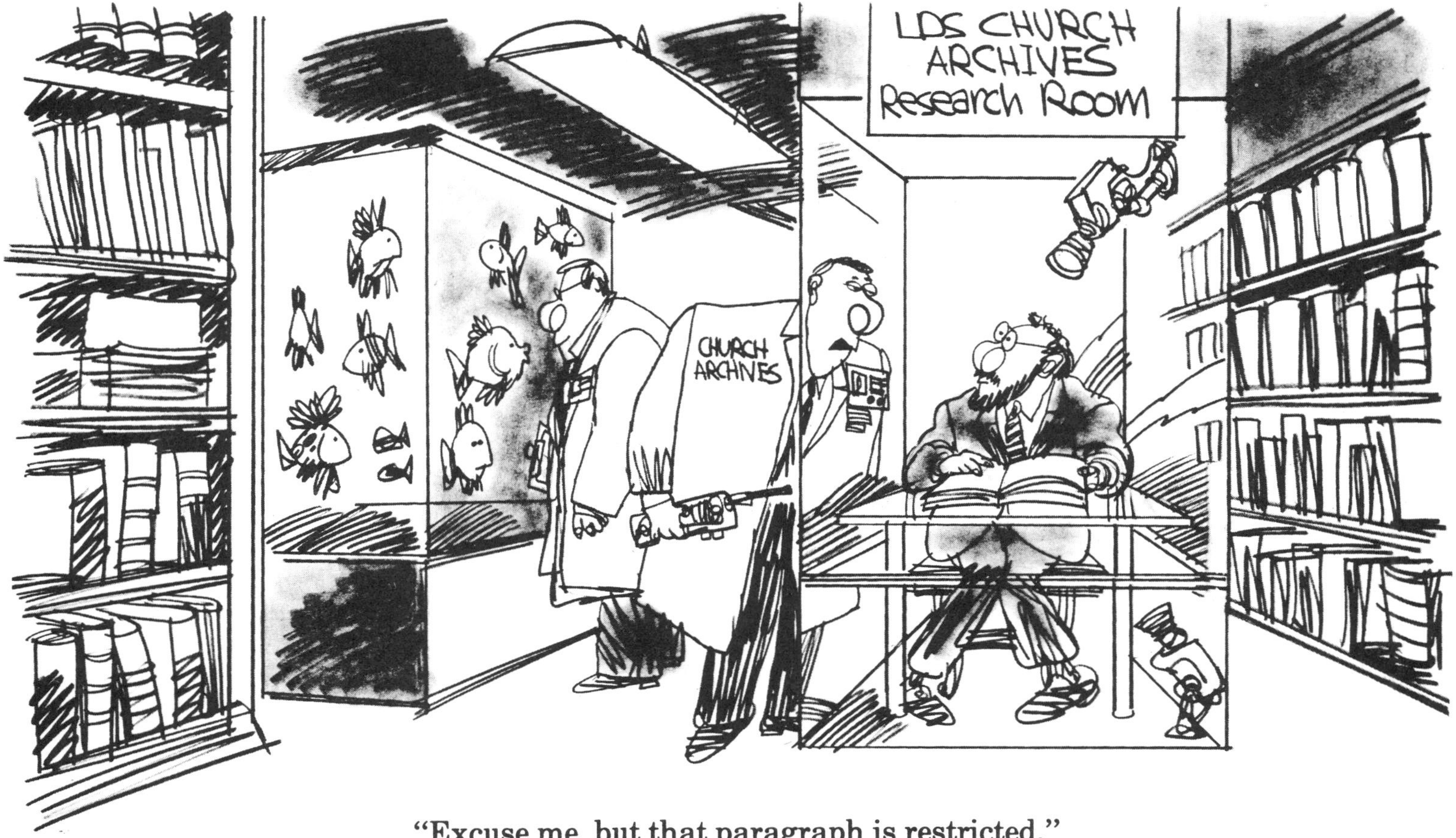
LDS CHURCH
ARCHIVES
Research Room
CHURCH
ARCHIVES

"Excuse me, but that paragraph is restricted."

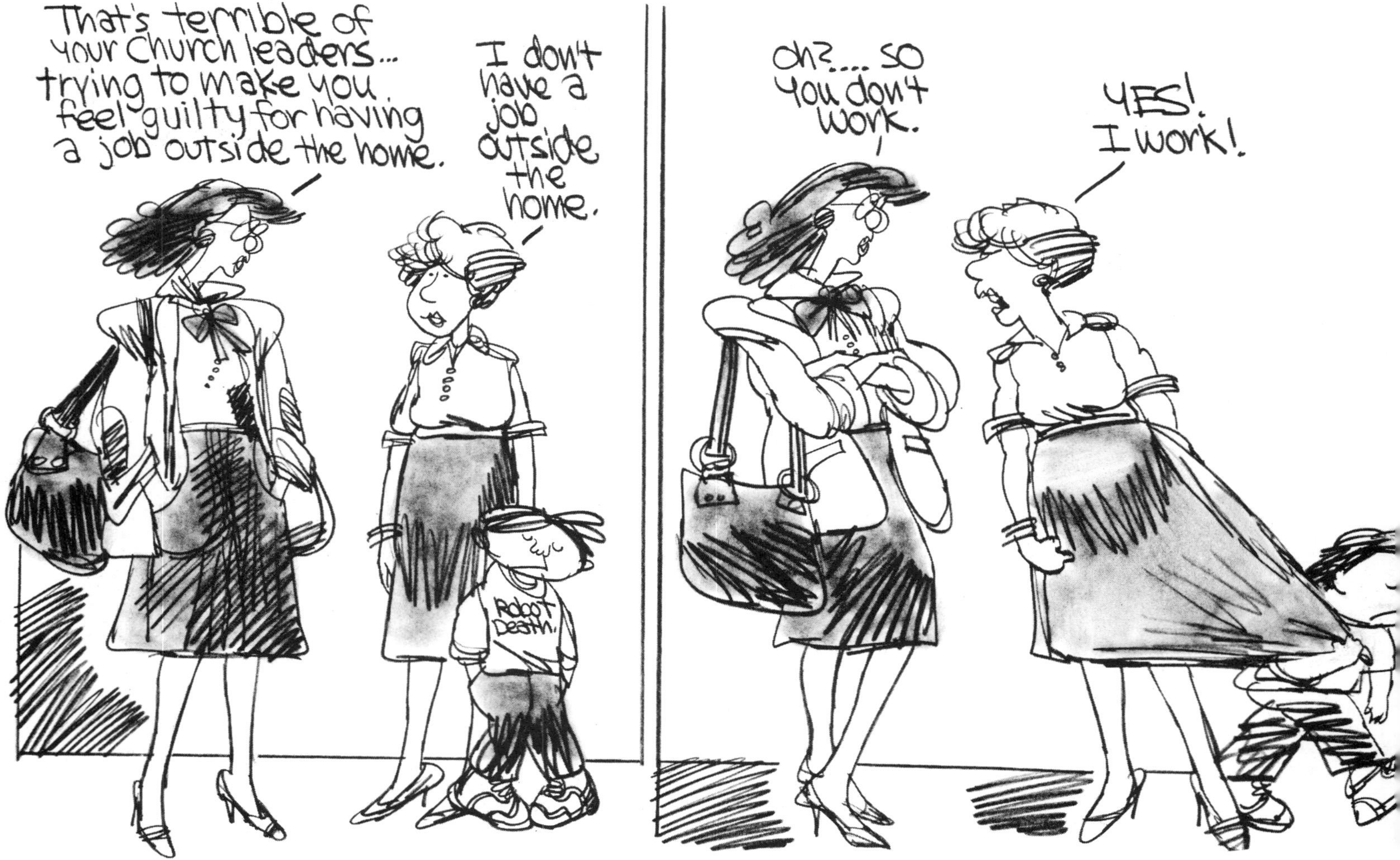

That's terrible of your Church leaders... trying to make you feel guilty for having a job outside the home.
I don't have a job outside the home.
Robot Death.
Oh?.... So you don't work.
YES! I work!

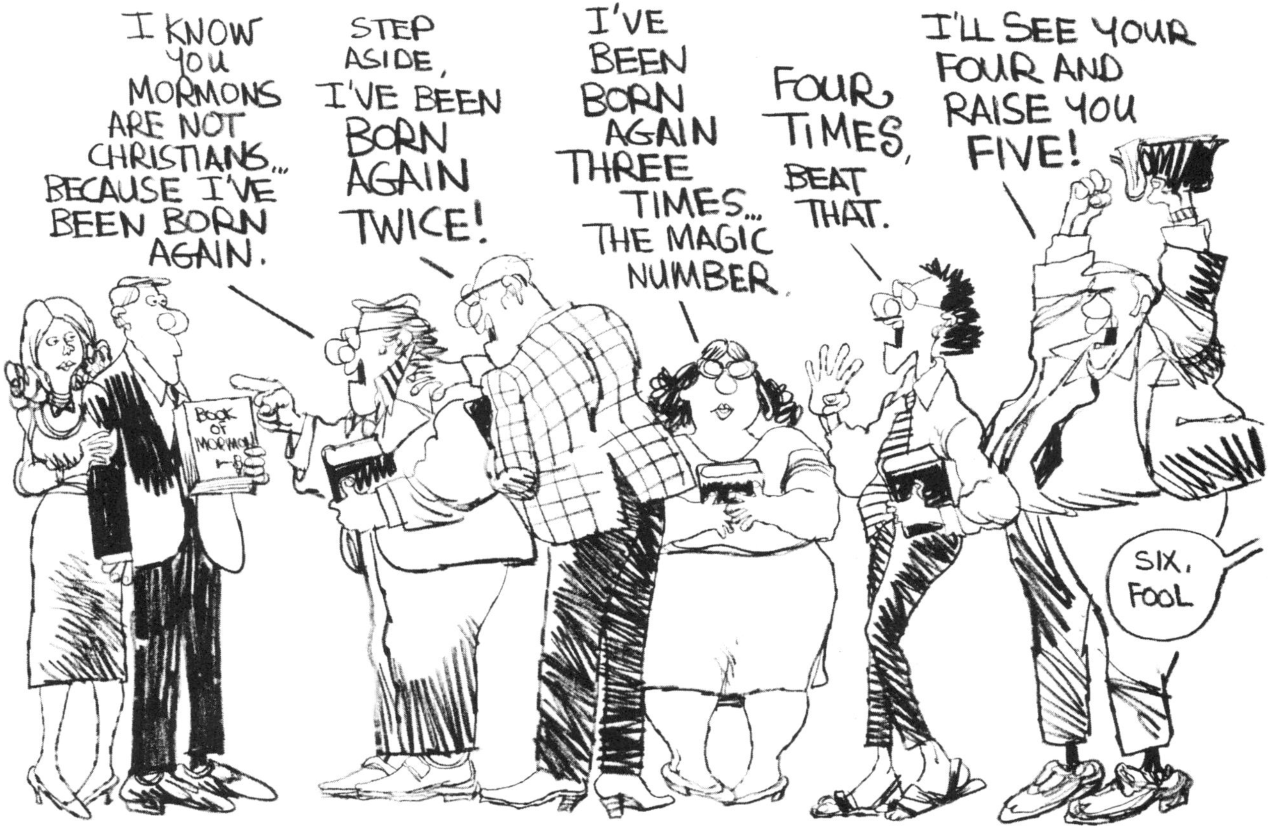
I KNOW YOU MORMONS ARE NOT CHRISTIANS... BECAUSE I'VE BEEN BORN AGAIN.
BOOK OF MORMON
STEP ASIDE, I'VE BEEN BORN AGAIN TWICE!
I'VE BEEN BORN AGAIN THREE TIMES... THE MAGIC NUMBER.
FOUR TIMES, BEAT THAT.
I'LL SEE YOUR FOUR AND RAISE YOU FIVE!
SIX, FOOL

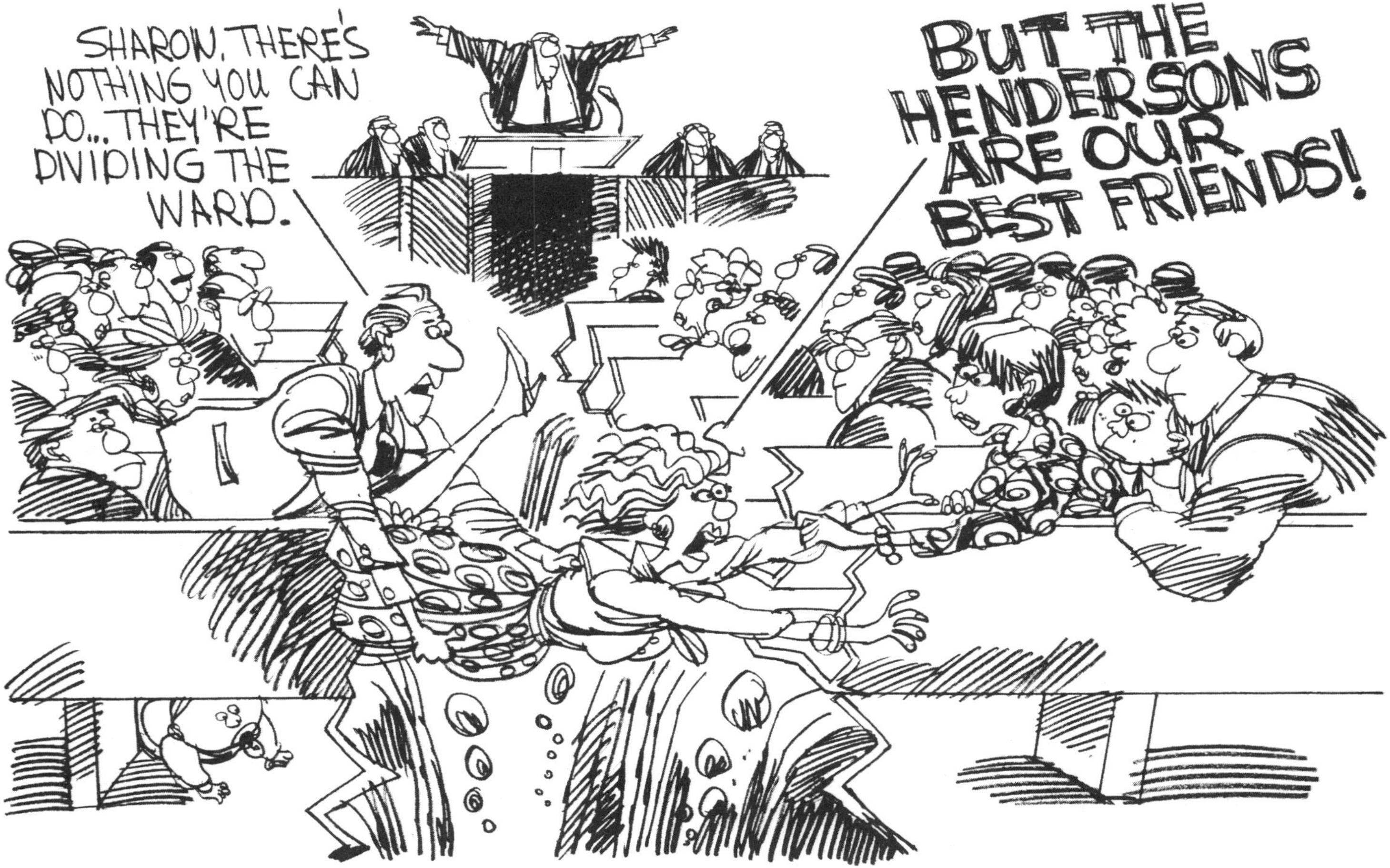
SHARON, THERE'S NOTHING YOU CAN DO... THEY'RE DIVIDING THE WARD.
BUT THE HENDERSONS ARE OUR BEST FRIENDS!

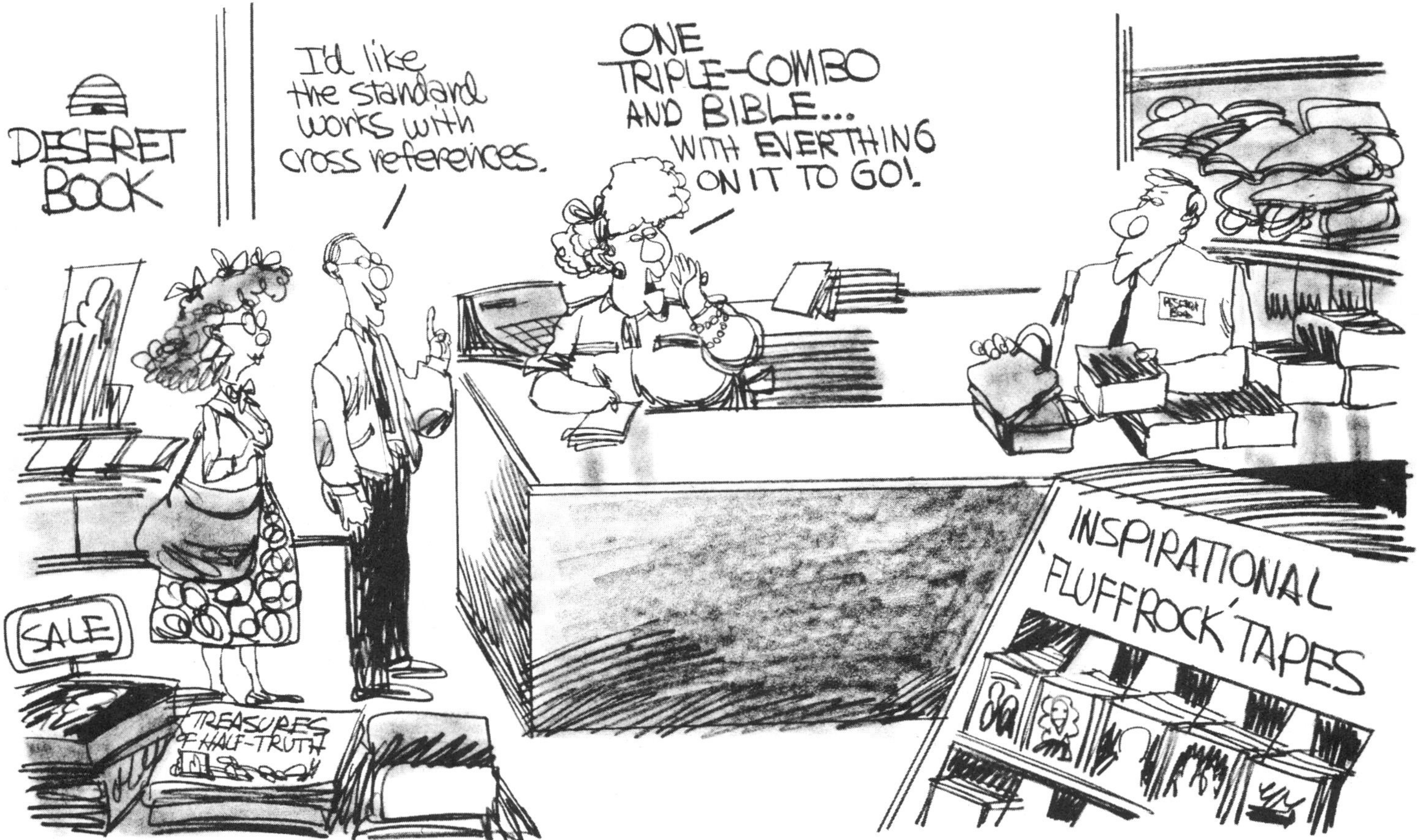
DESERET BOOK
I'd like the standard works with cross references.
ONE TRIPLE-COMBO AND BIBLE... WITH EVERTHING ON IT TO GO!
SALE
TREASURES OF HALF-TRUTH
INSPIRATIONAL 'FLUFFROCK' TAPES

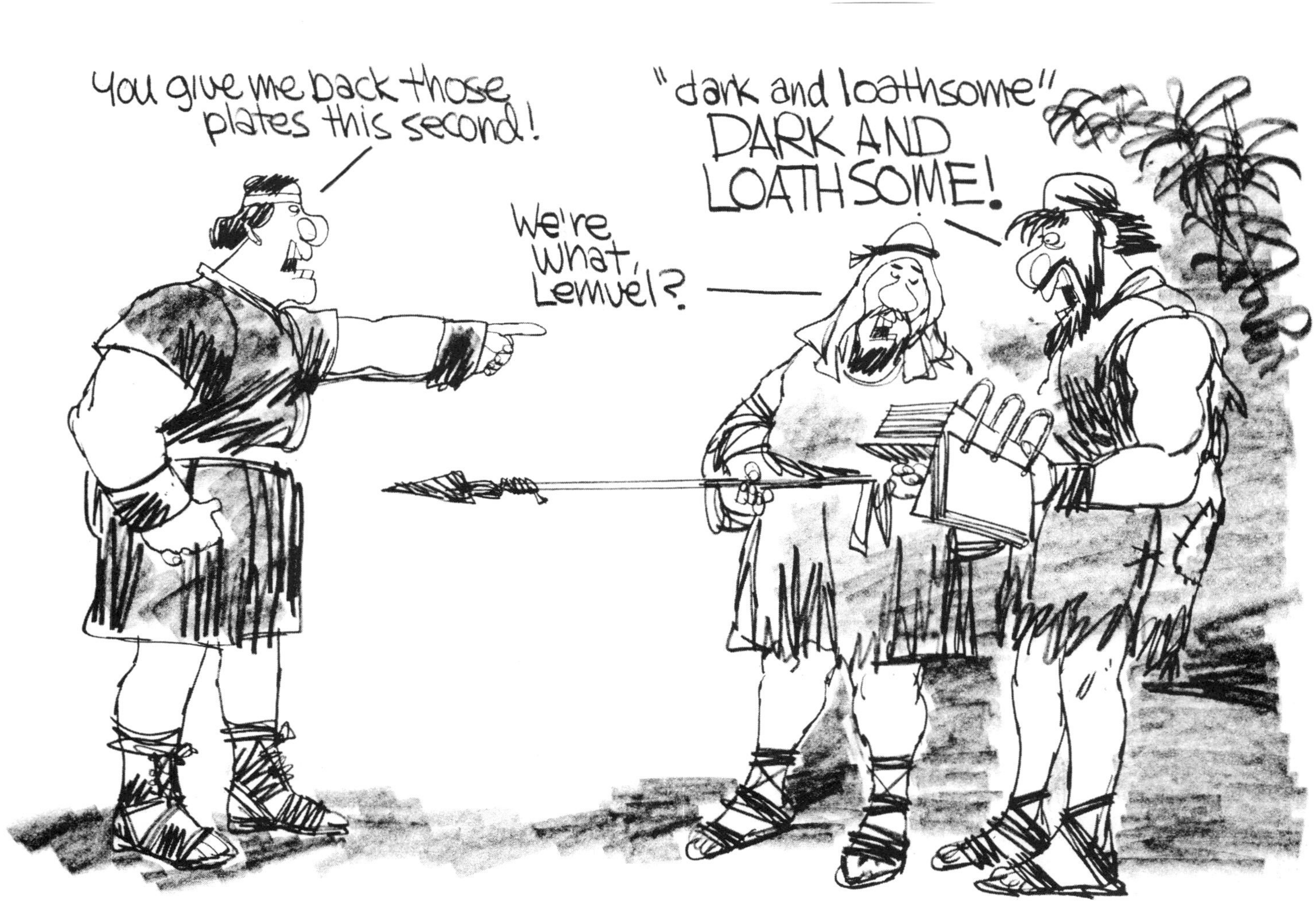
You give me back those plates this second!
We're what, Lemuel?
"dark and loathsome"
DARK AND LOATHSOME!

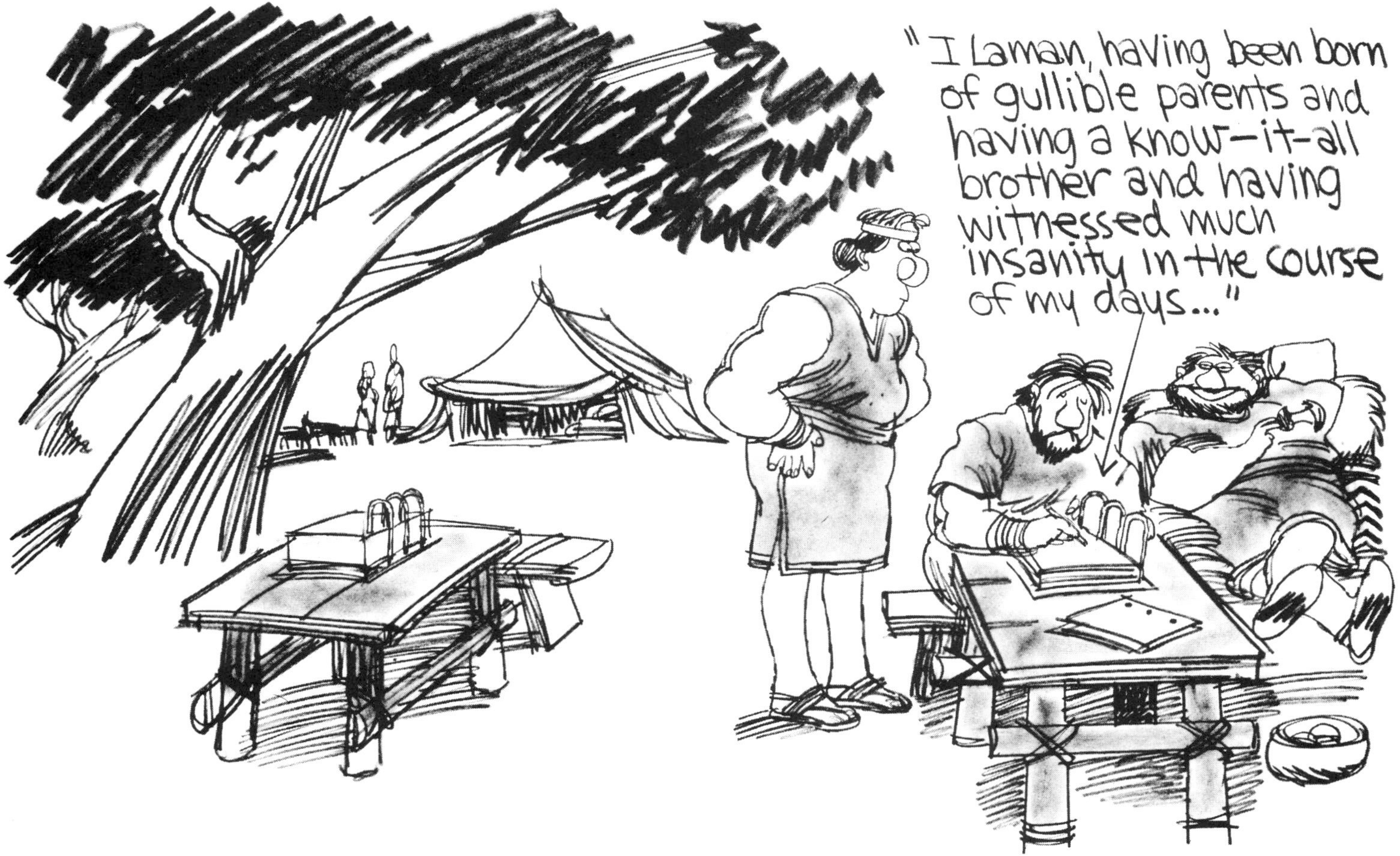
"I Laman, having been born of gullible parents and having a know-it-all brother and having witnessed much insanity in the course of my days..."

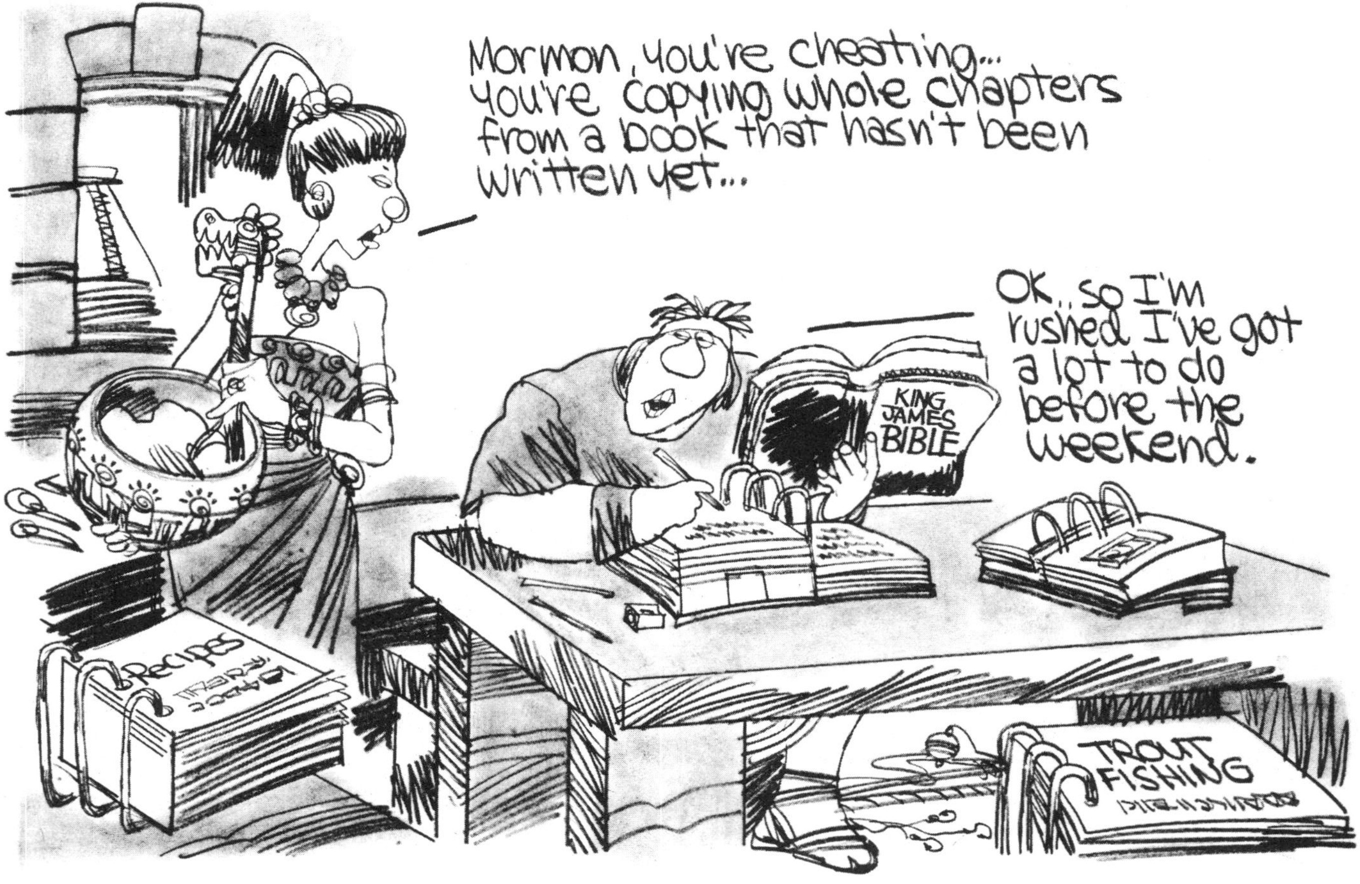

Mormon, you're cheating... you're copying whole chapters from a book that hasn't been written yet...
OK, so I'm rushed I've got a lot to do before the weekend.
KING JAMES BIBLE
RECIPES
TROUT FISHING

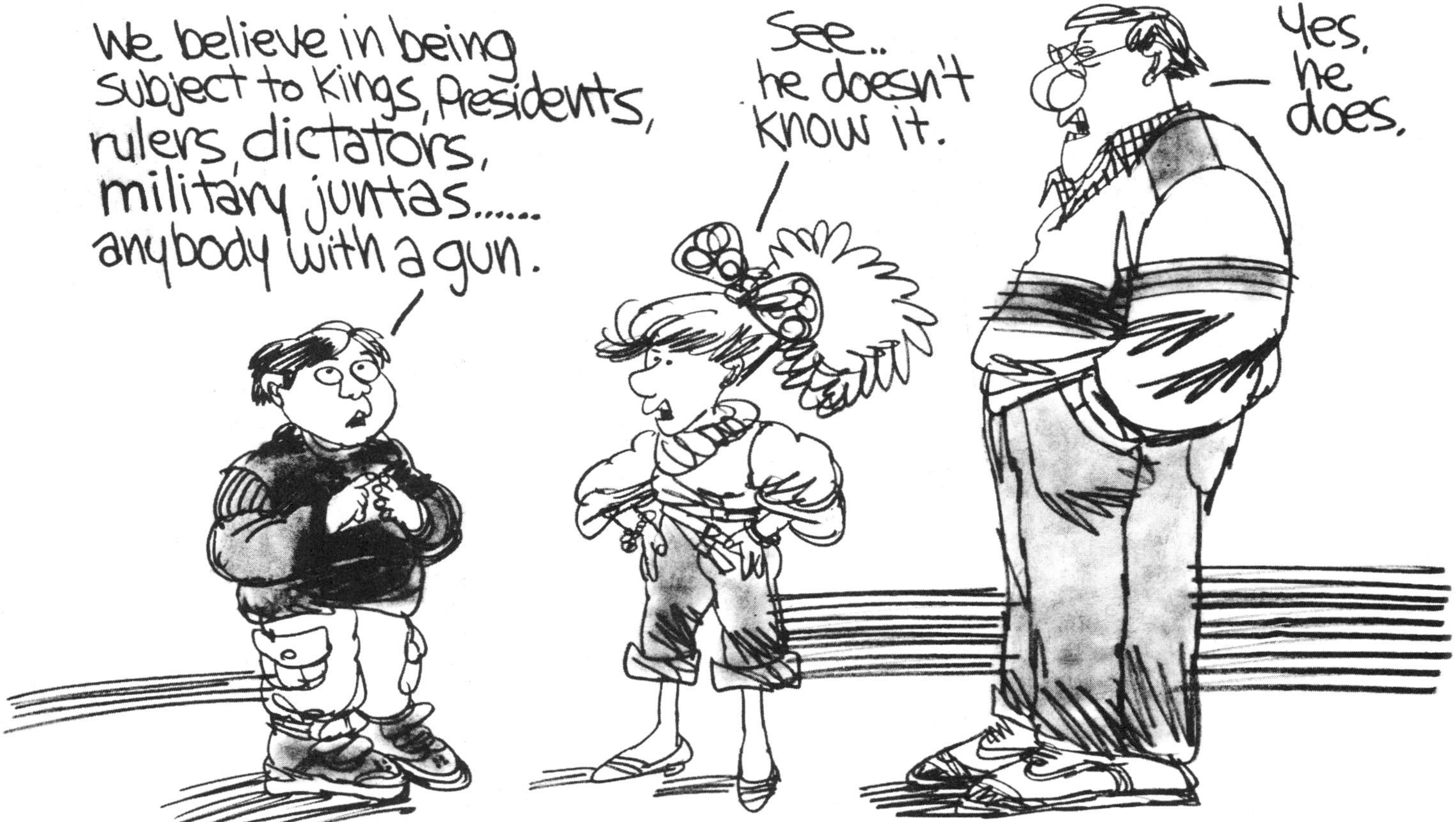
We believe in being subject to kings, presidents, rulers, dictators, military juntas...... anybody with a gun.
See... he doesn't know it.
Yes, he does.

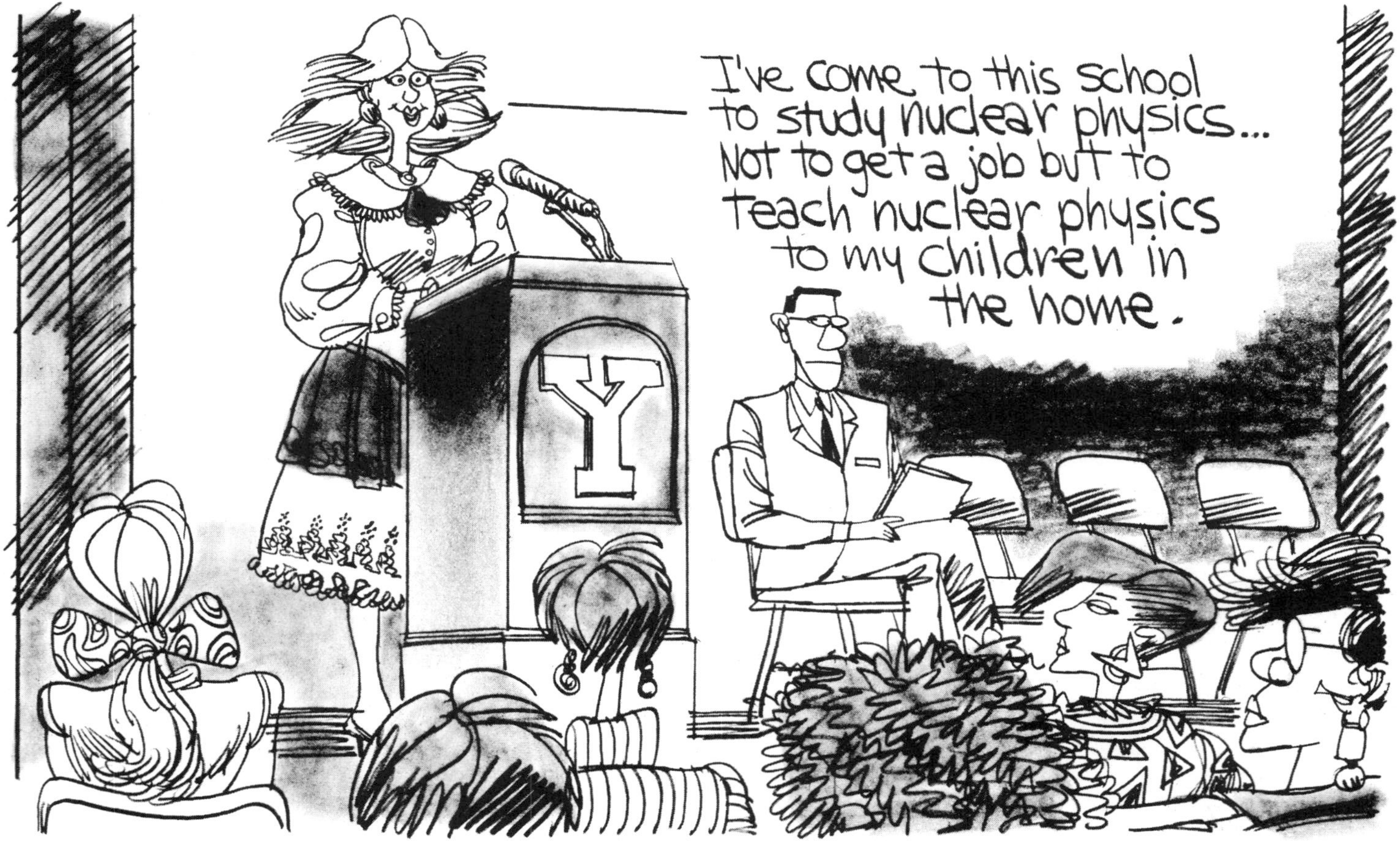
I've come to this school to study nuclear physics... Not to get a job but to teach nuclear physics to my children in the home.

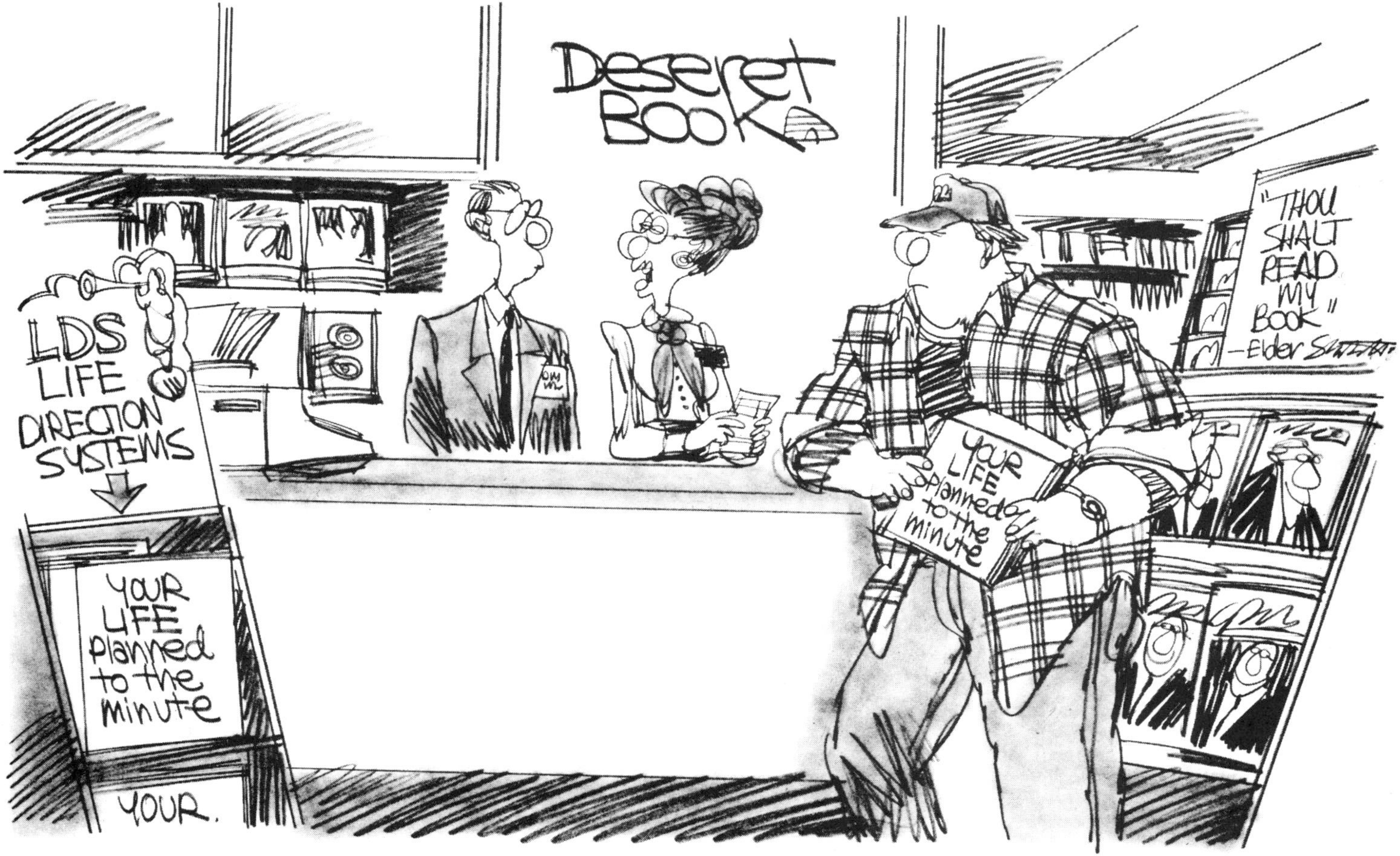
Deseret Book
LDS LIFE DIRECTION SYSTEMS
YOUR LIFE planned to the minute
YOUR.
"THOU SHALT READ MY BOOK"
YOUR LIFE planned to the minute

"He says he got it for his birthday and wants to exchange it for a book on fly fishing."

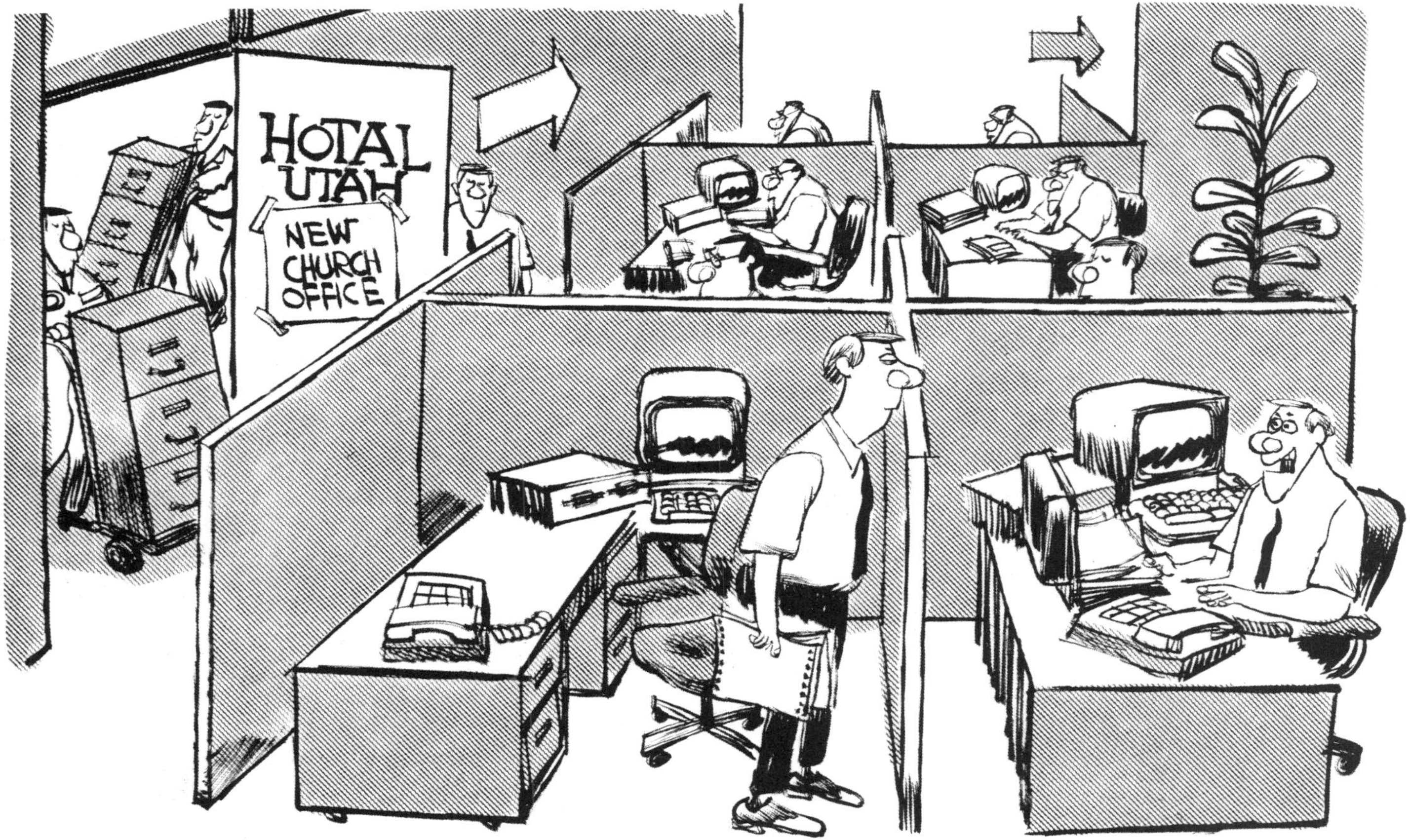
HOTAL UTAH
NEW CHURCH OFFICE

"... it just occurred to me — this cubicle is where my wife and I spent our honeymoon!"

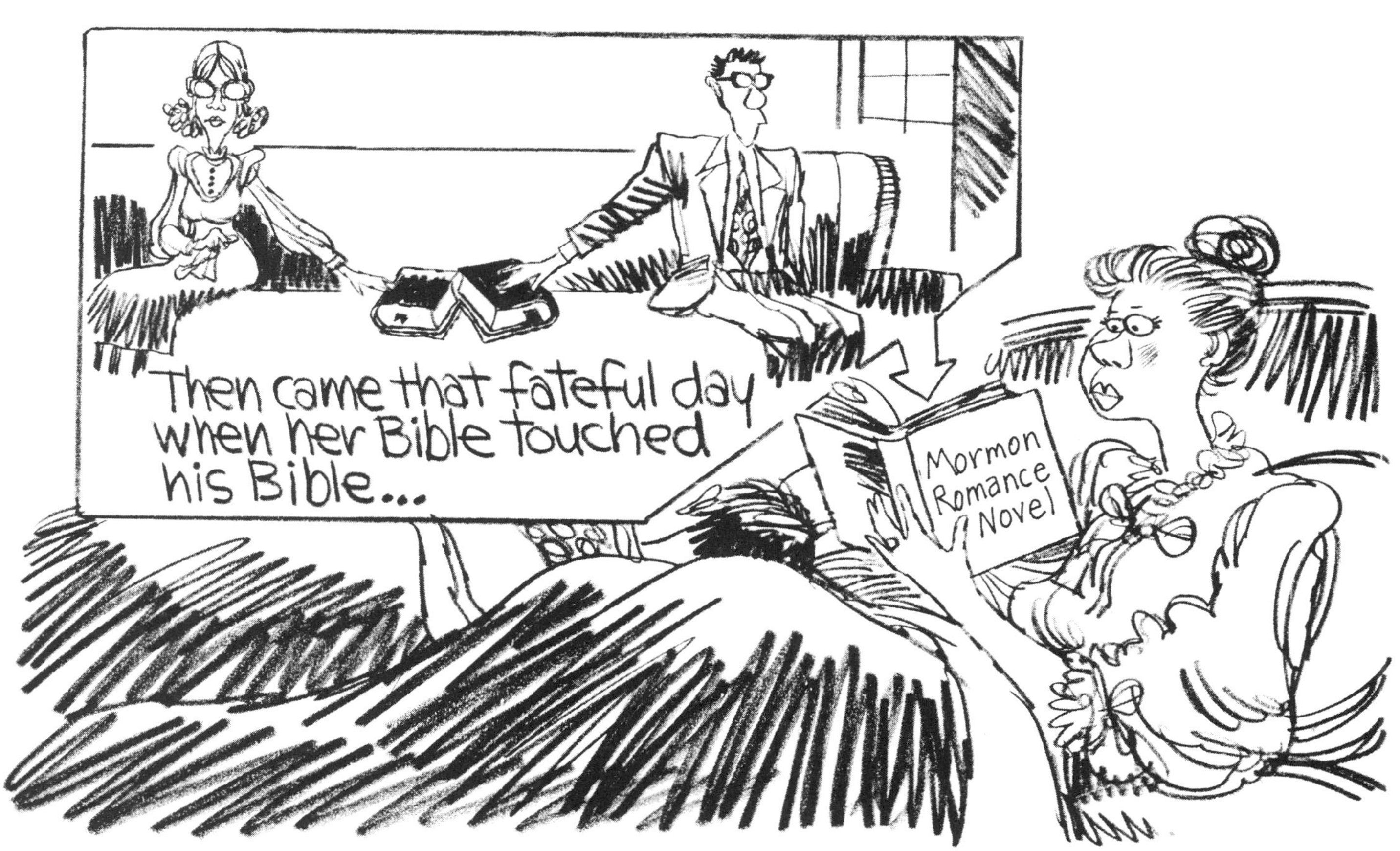
Then came that fateful day when her Bible touched his Bible...
Mormon Romance Novel

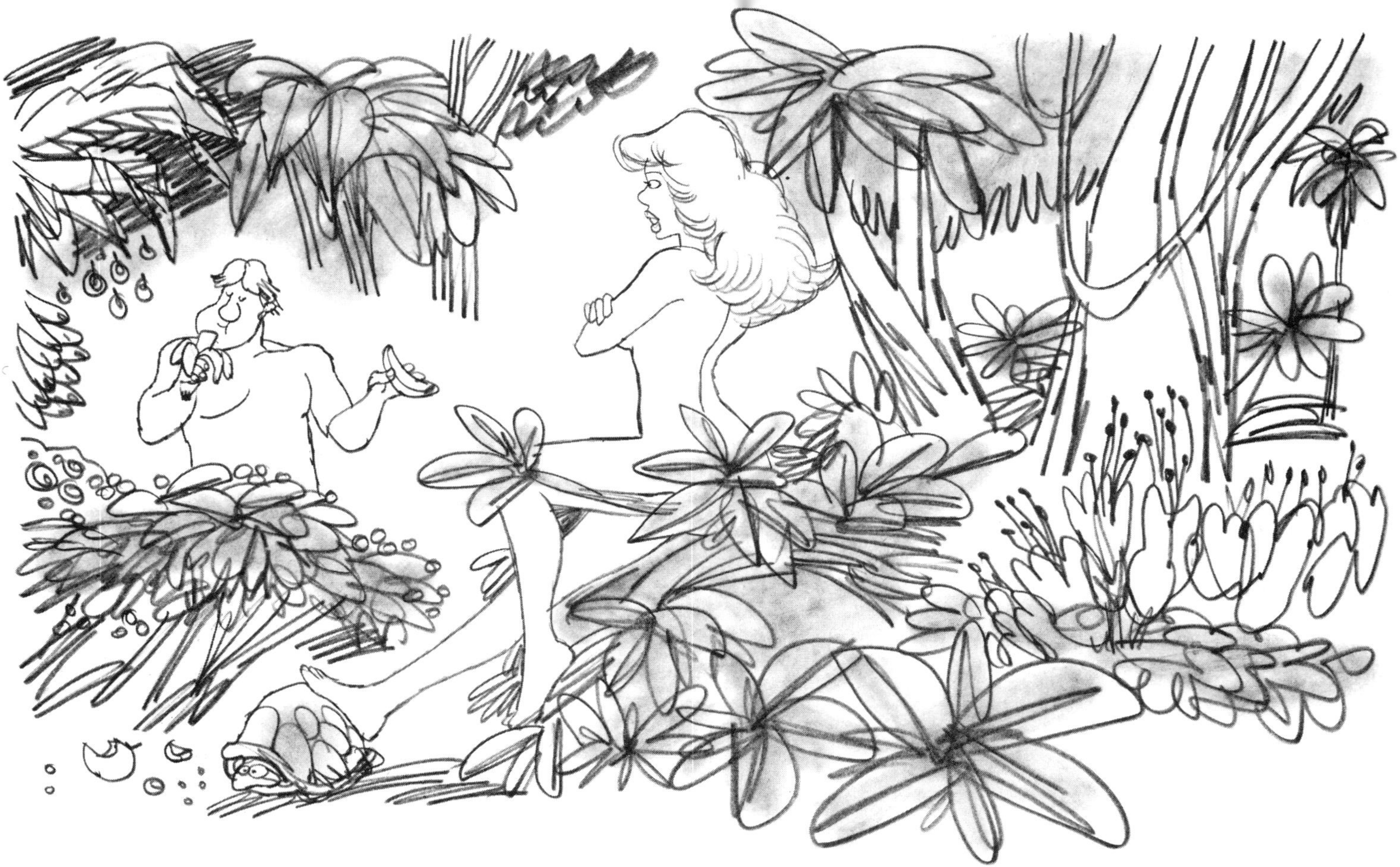

“Adam, let’s do something different tonight. Let’s get dressed and go out to eat.”

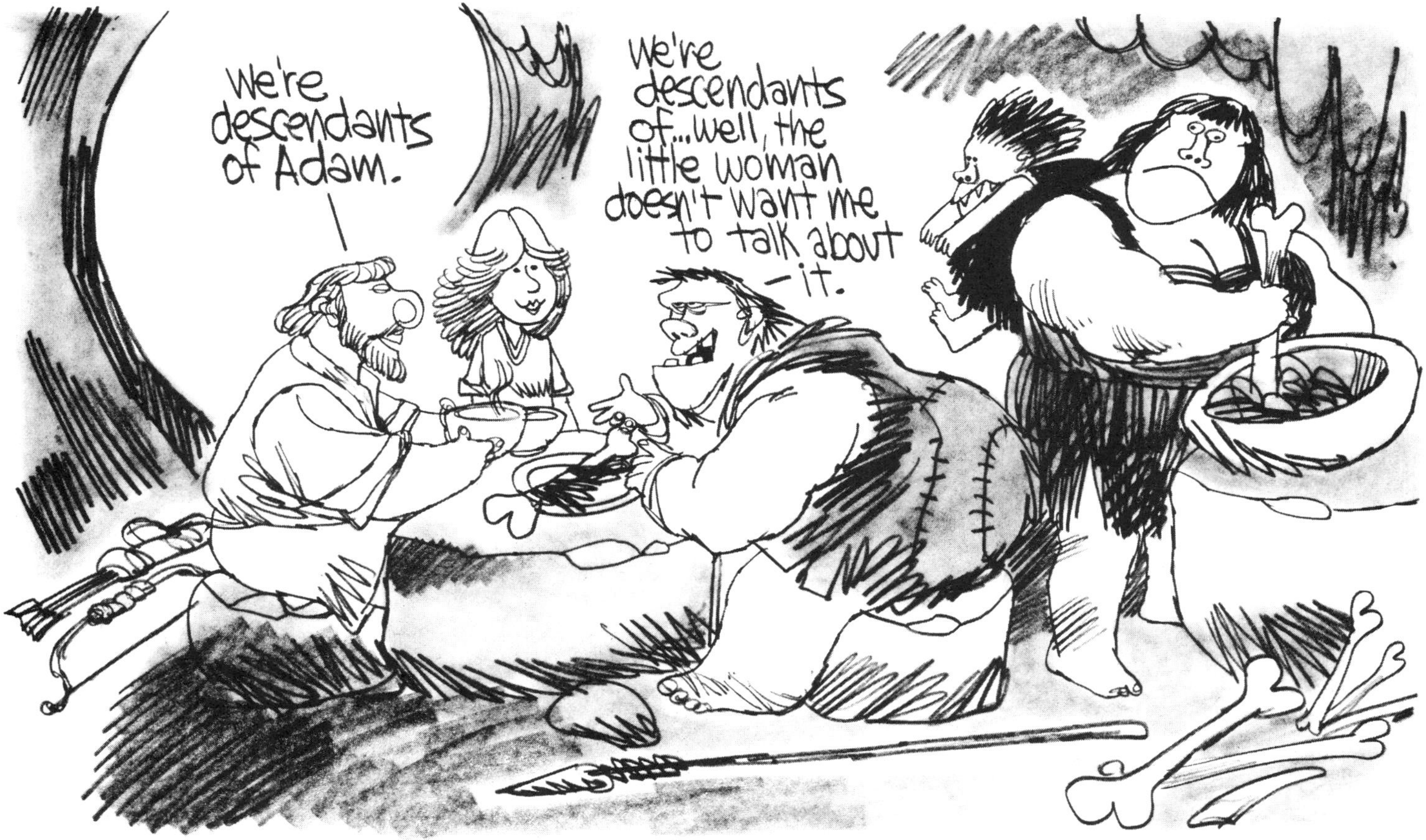
We're descendants of Adam.
We're descendants of...well, the little woman doesn't want me to talk about it.

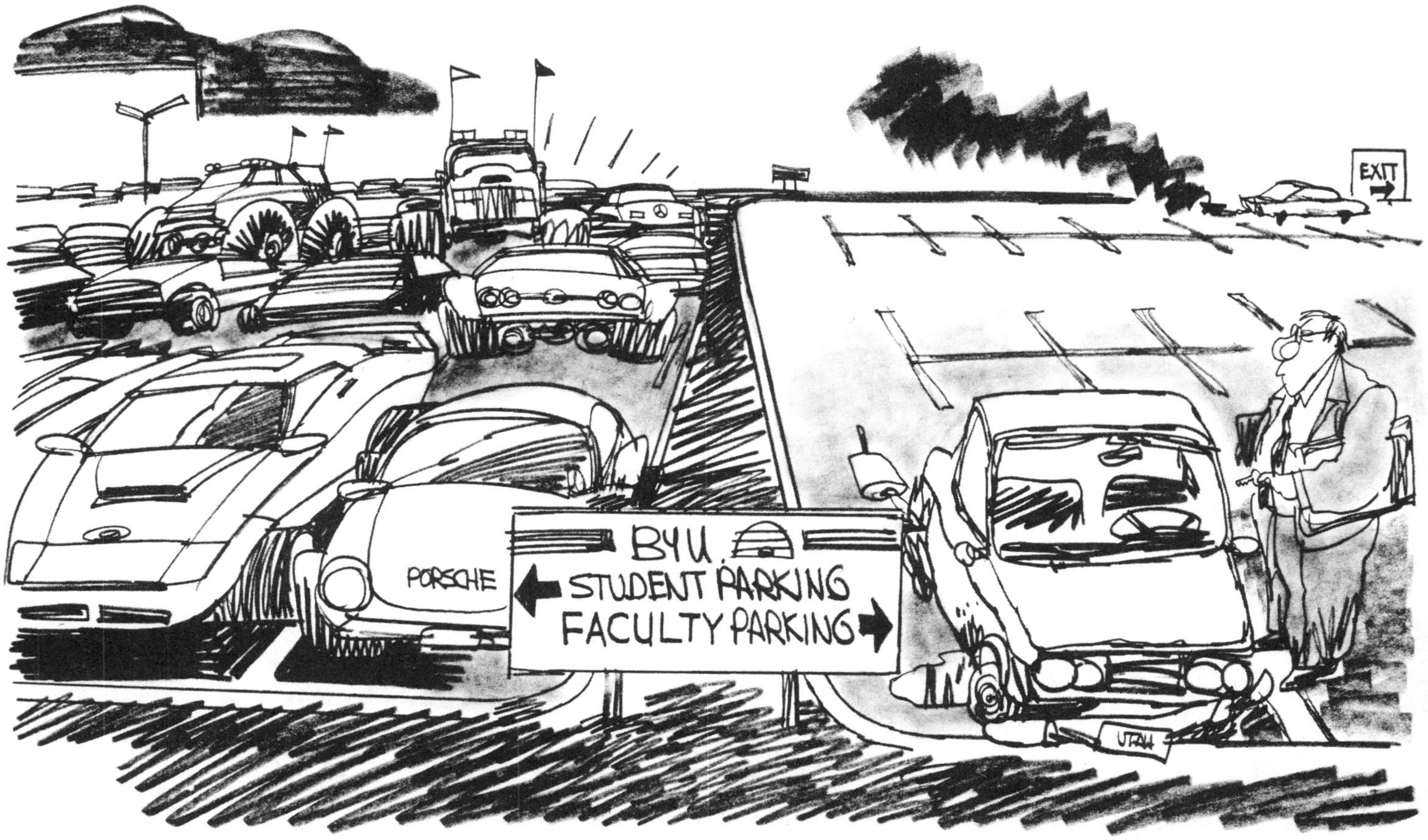
EXIT
PORSCHE
BYU
STUDENT PARKING
FACULTY PARKING
UTAH

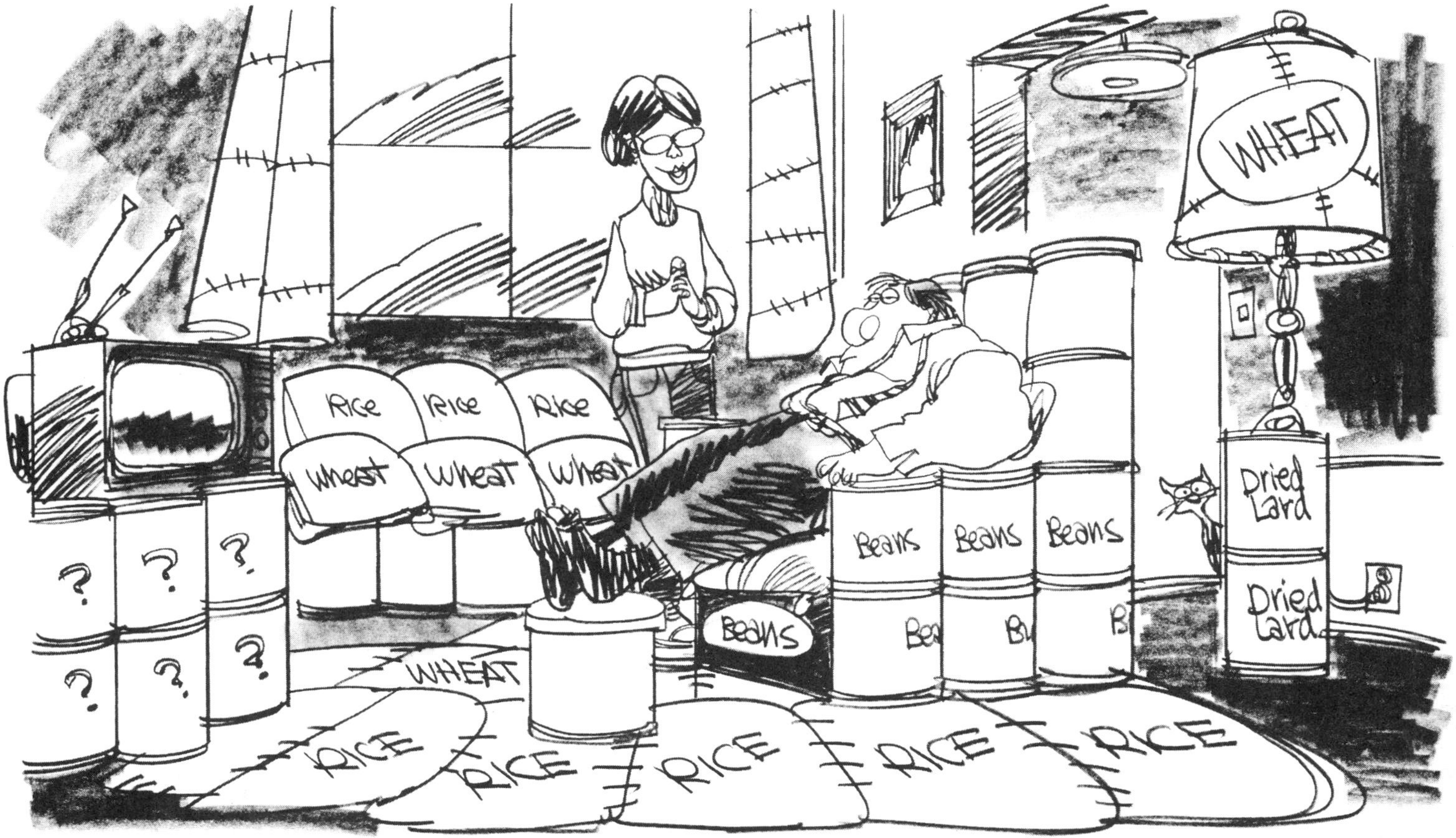
WHEAT
Rice
Rice
Rice
Wheat
Wheat
Beans
Beans
Beans
Dried Lard
Dried Lard
Beans
WHEAT
RICE
RICE
RICE
RICE
RICE

"You see, everything has a special purpose — even this fifteen-year-old food storage."

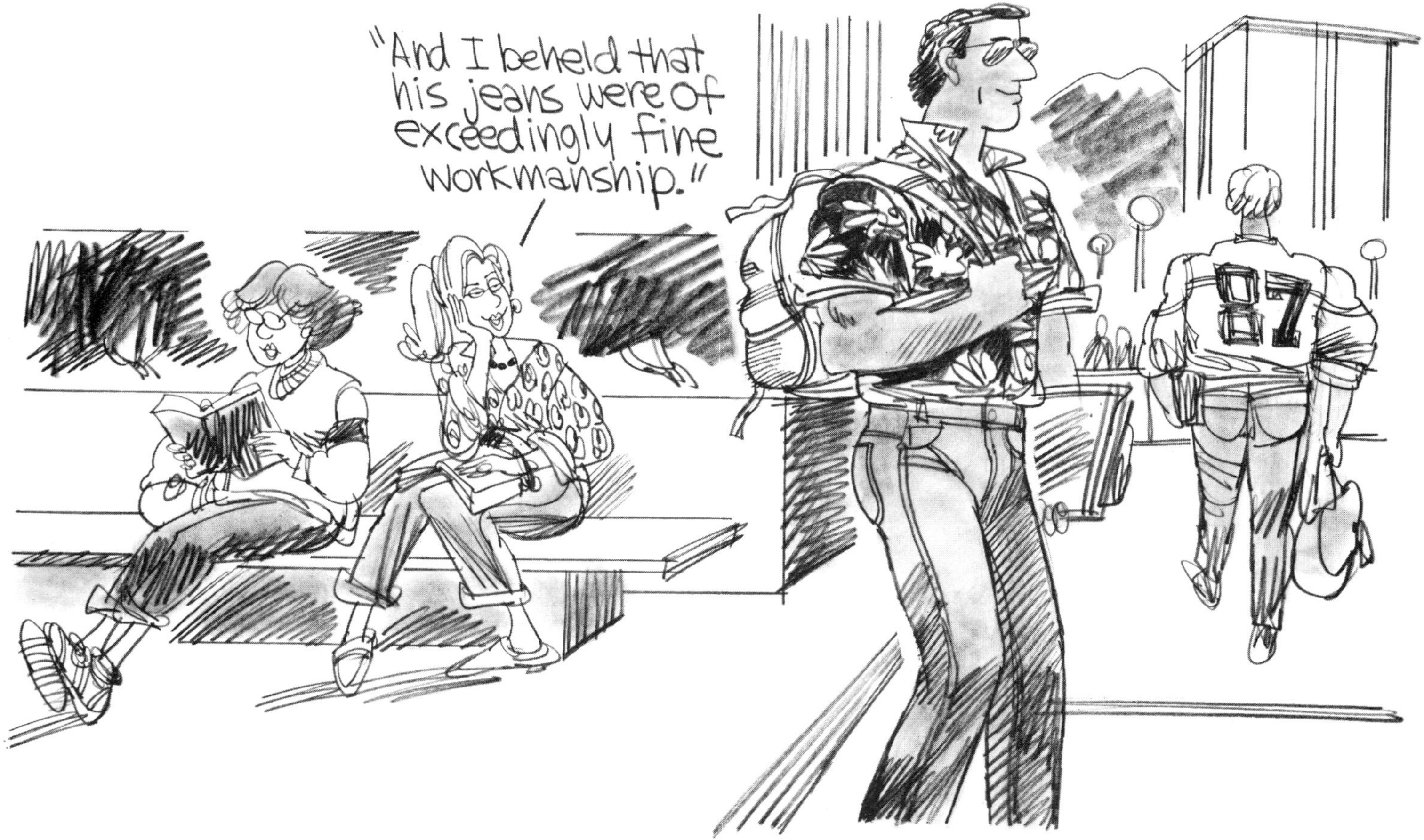
"And I beheld that his jeans were of exceedingly fine workmanship."
87

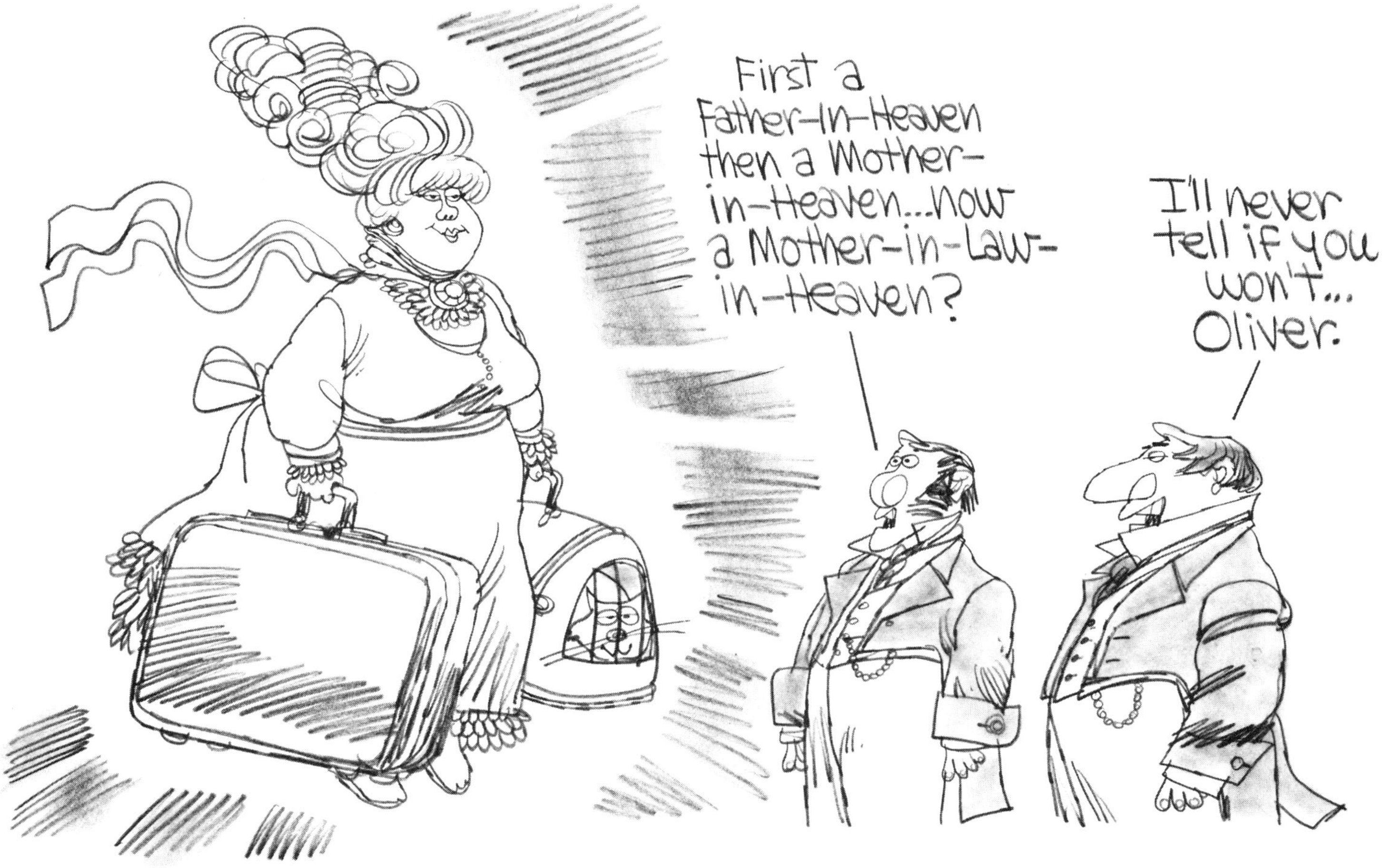
First a Father-In-Heaven then a Mother-in-Heaven...now a Mother-in-Law-in-Heaven?
I'll never tell if you won't... Oliver.

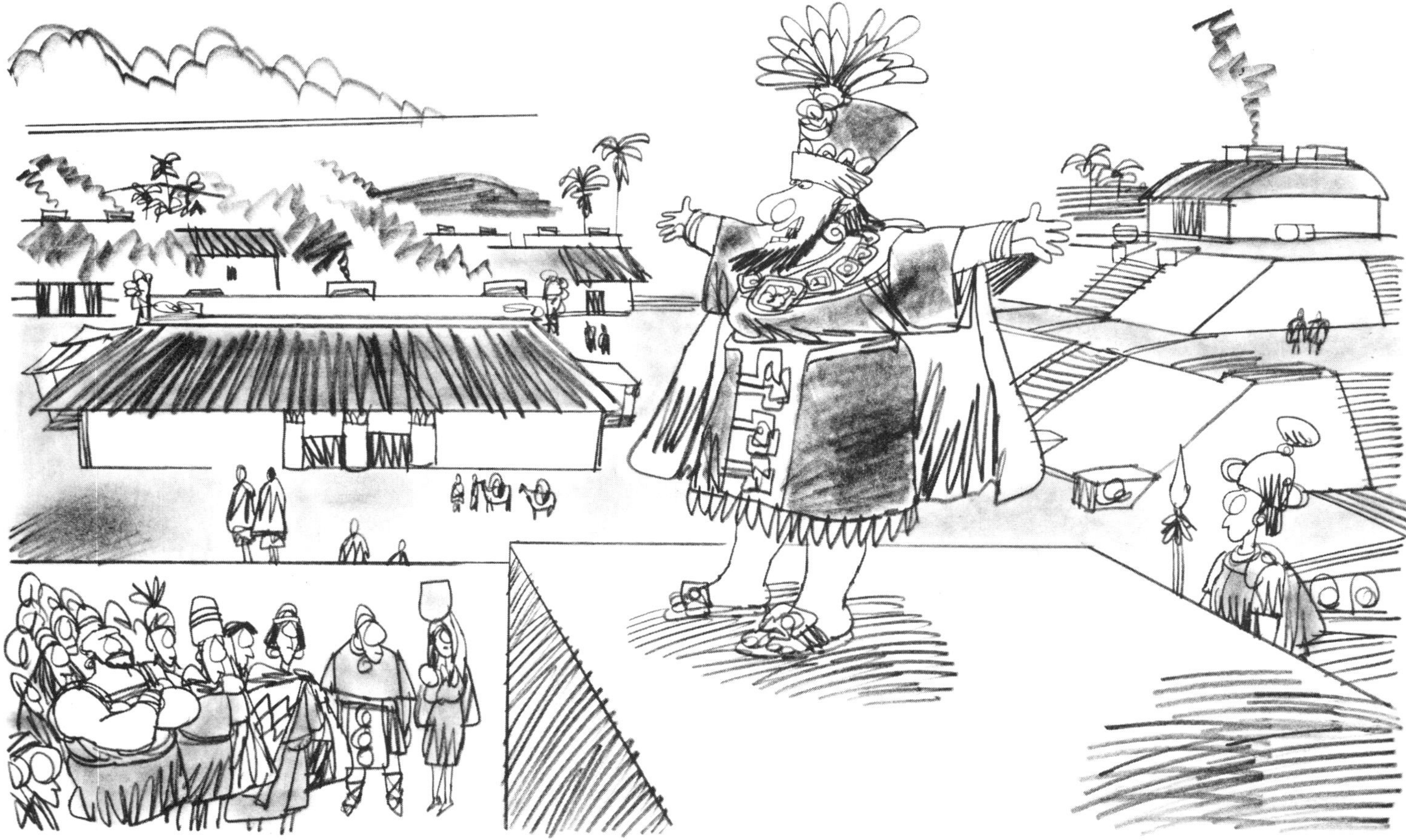

"As your prophet, I have labored with mine own hands not to be a burden unto you . . .
. . . laboring on the board of directors of Zarahemla Fuel Supply."

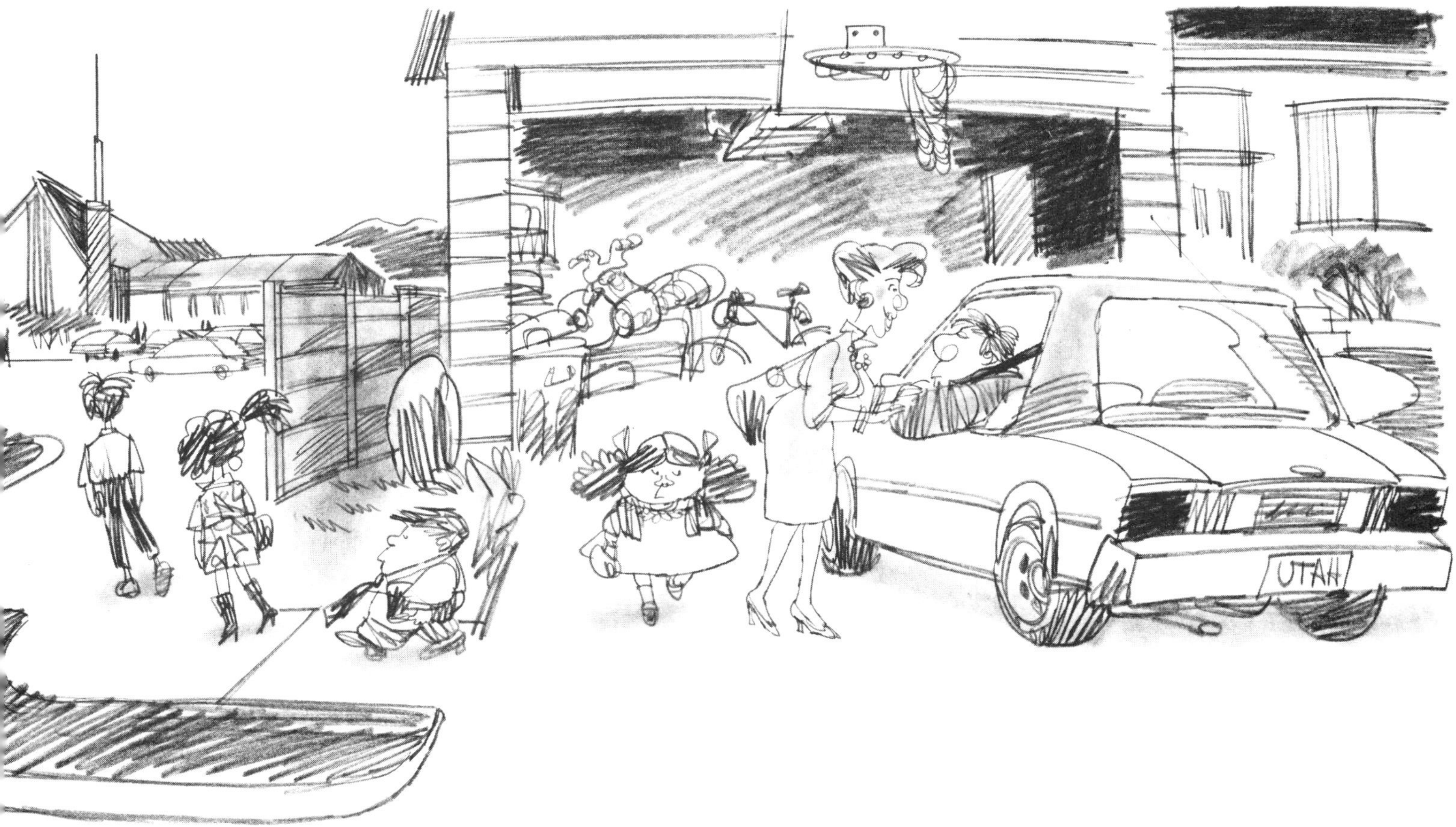
UTAH

"Dear, it's such a nice day. Let's walk to church."

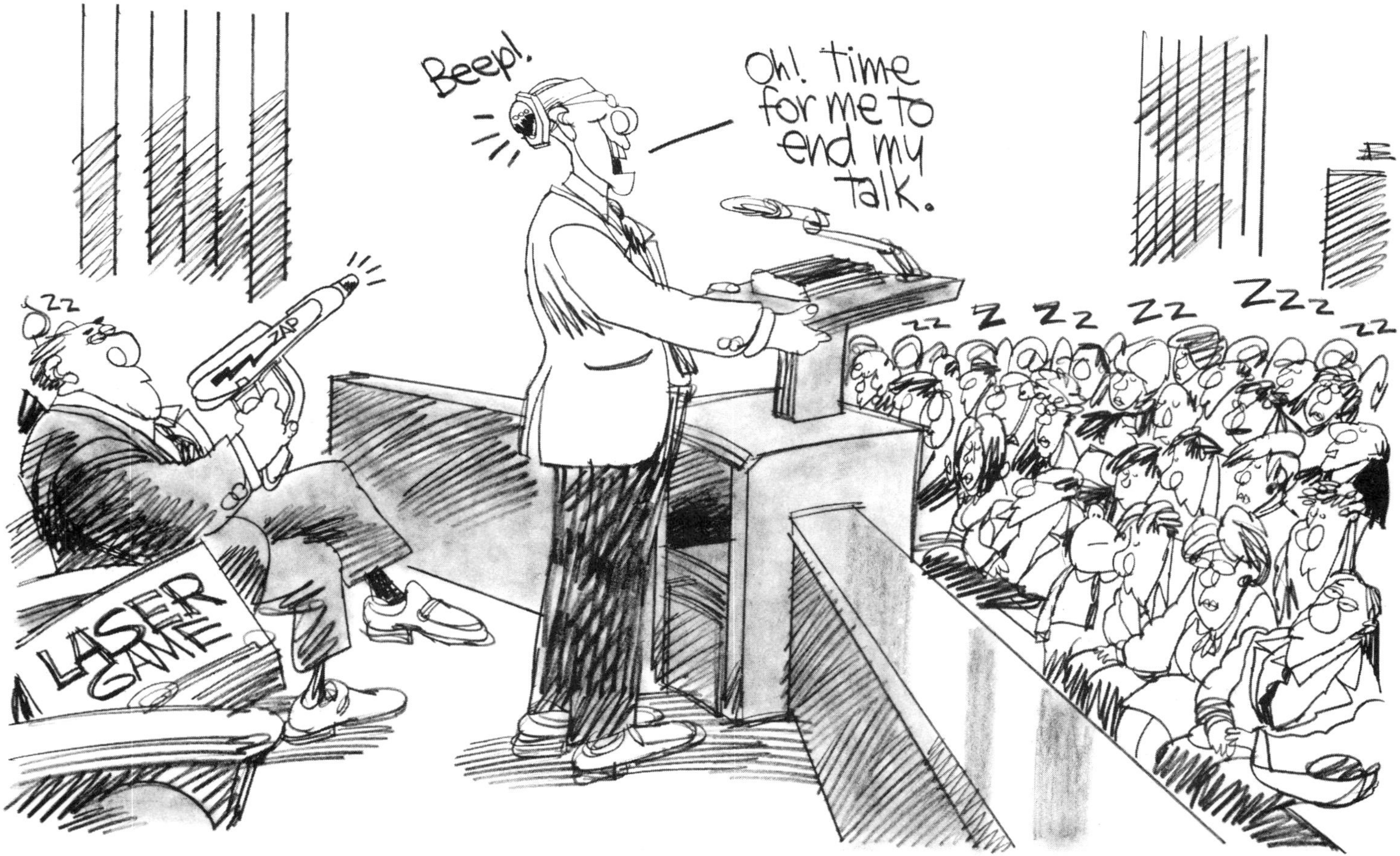
Beep!
Oh! time for me to end my talk.
ZAP
LASER GAME
Z Z Z

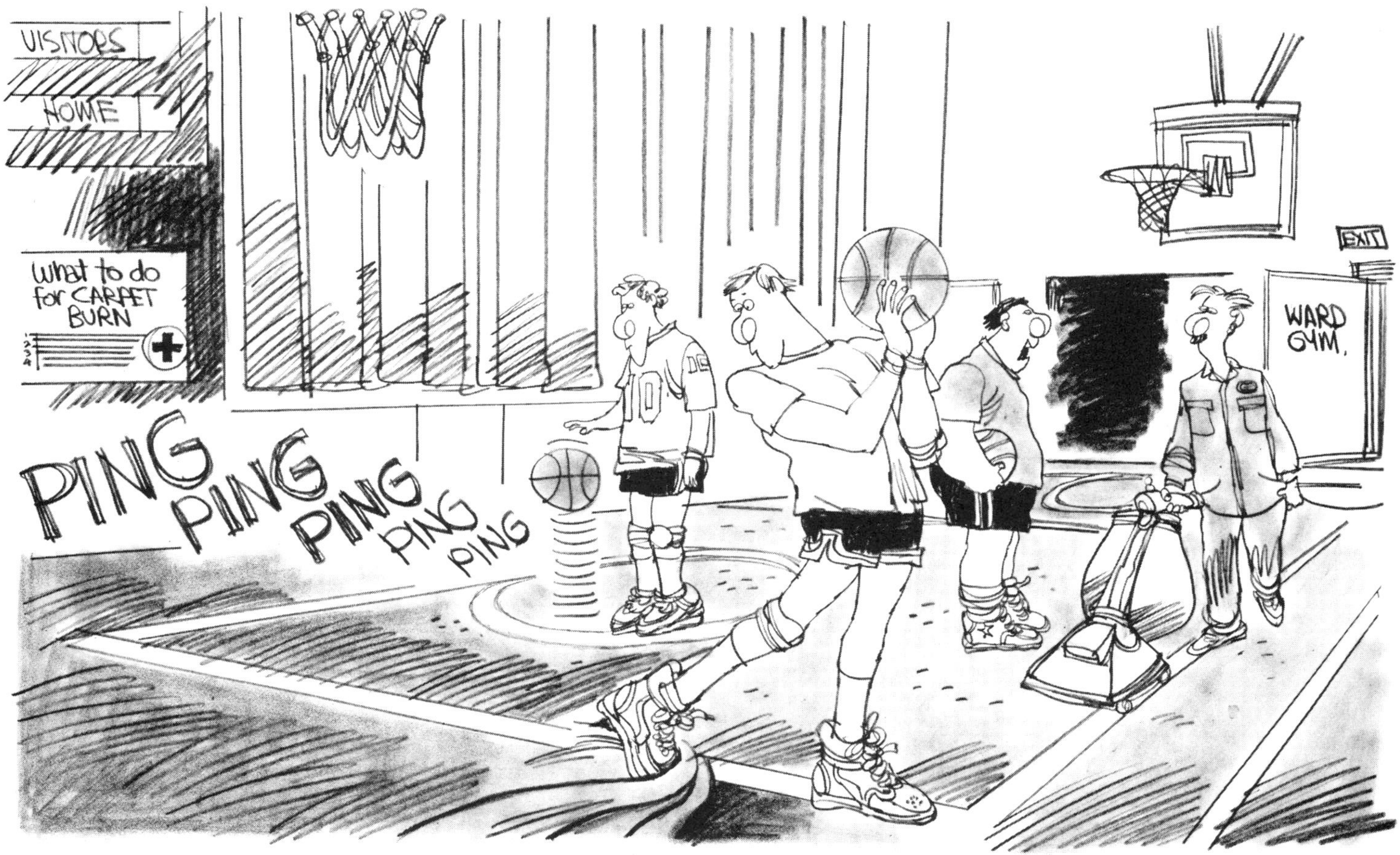
VISITORS
HOME
what to do for CARPET BURN
EXIT
WARD GYM
PING
PING
PING
PING
PING

"Couldn't you wait to vacuum the carpet until *after* the game?"

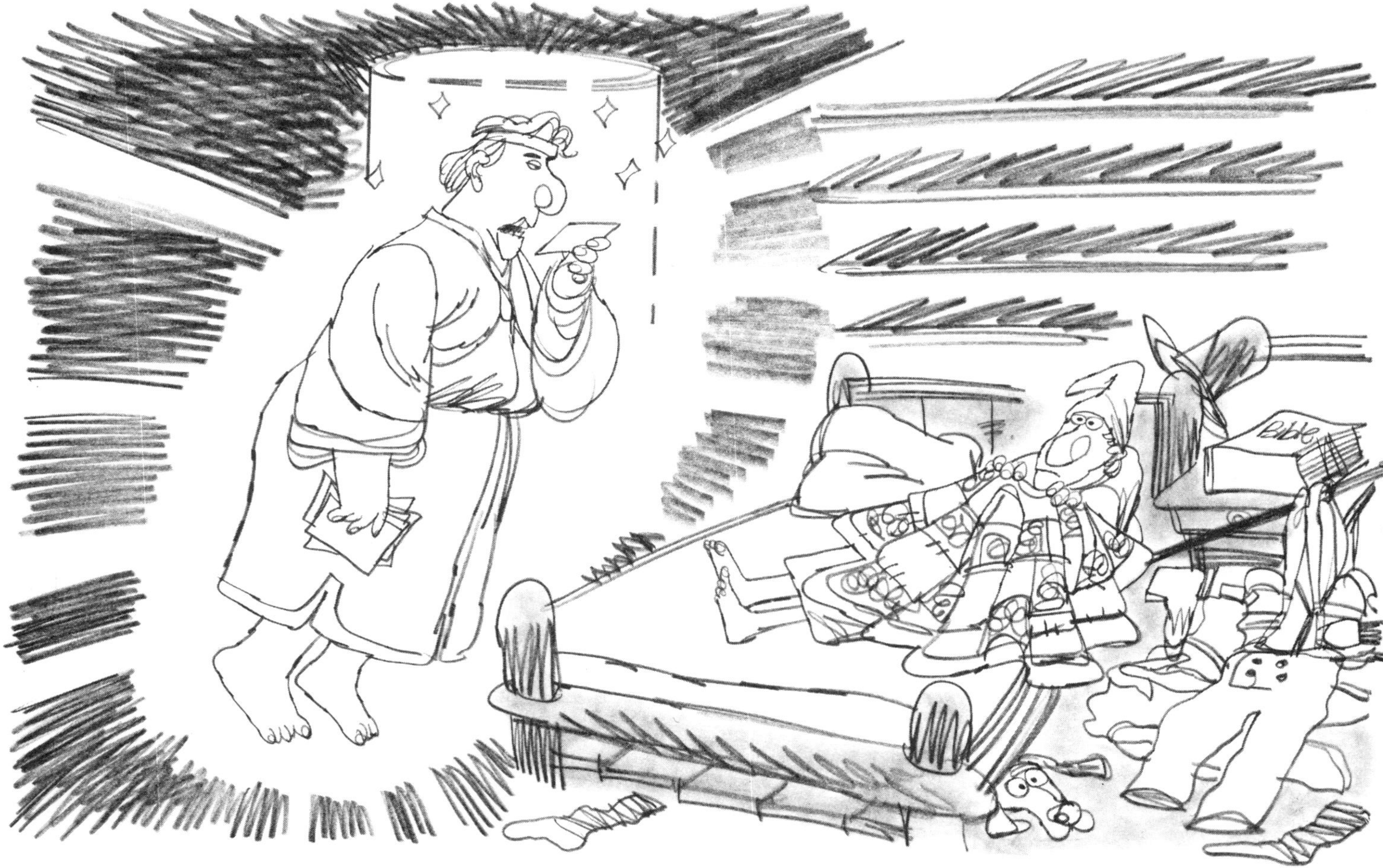
Bible

"And you shall find the plates wrapped in swaddling clothes . . . lying in a manger? Hmmm . . . that doesn't sound right."

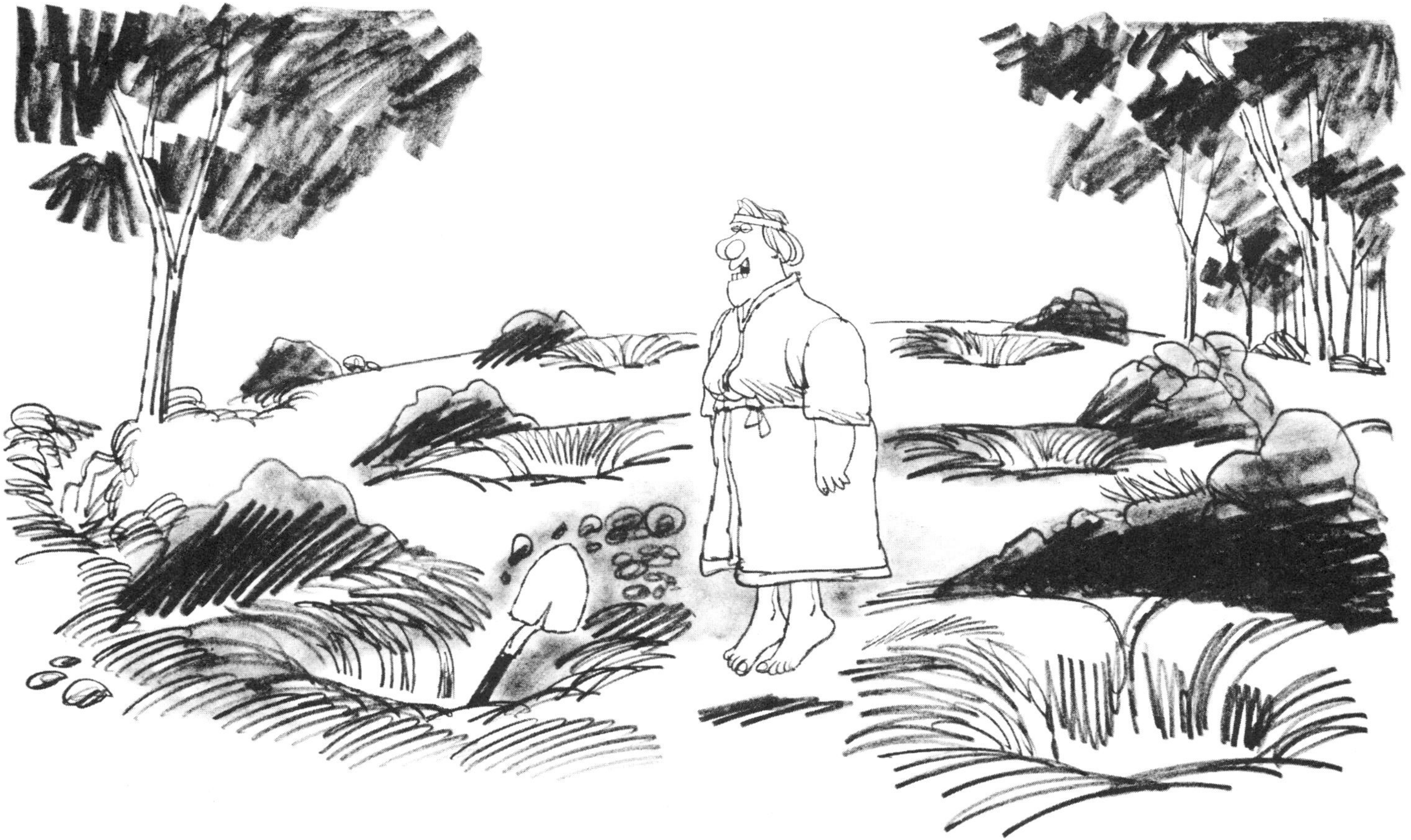

“I’m sorry Joseph, but after fifteen hundred years everything looks different.”

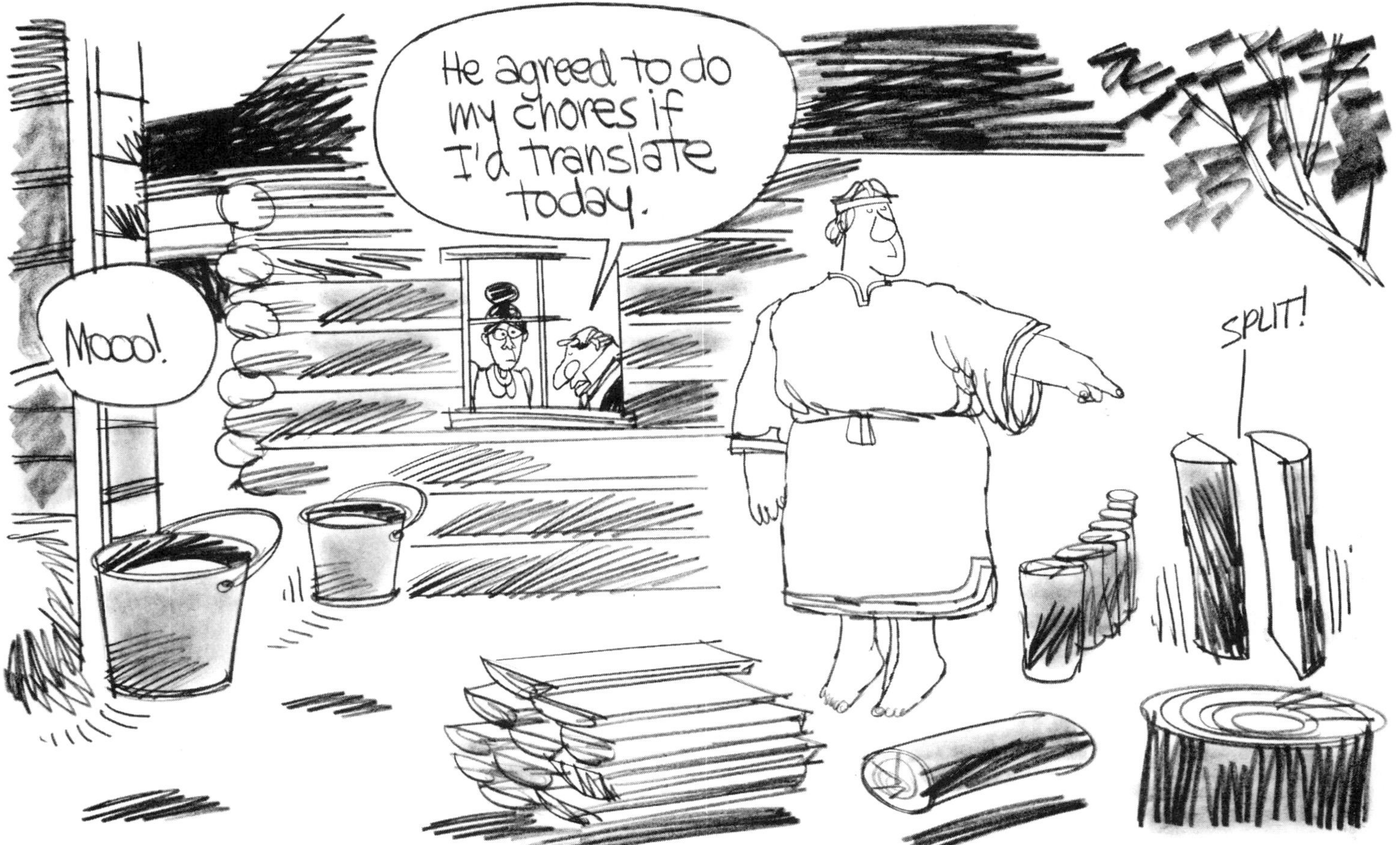

Moooo!
He agreed to do my chores if I'd translate today.
SPLIT!

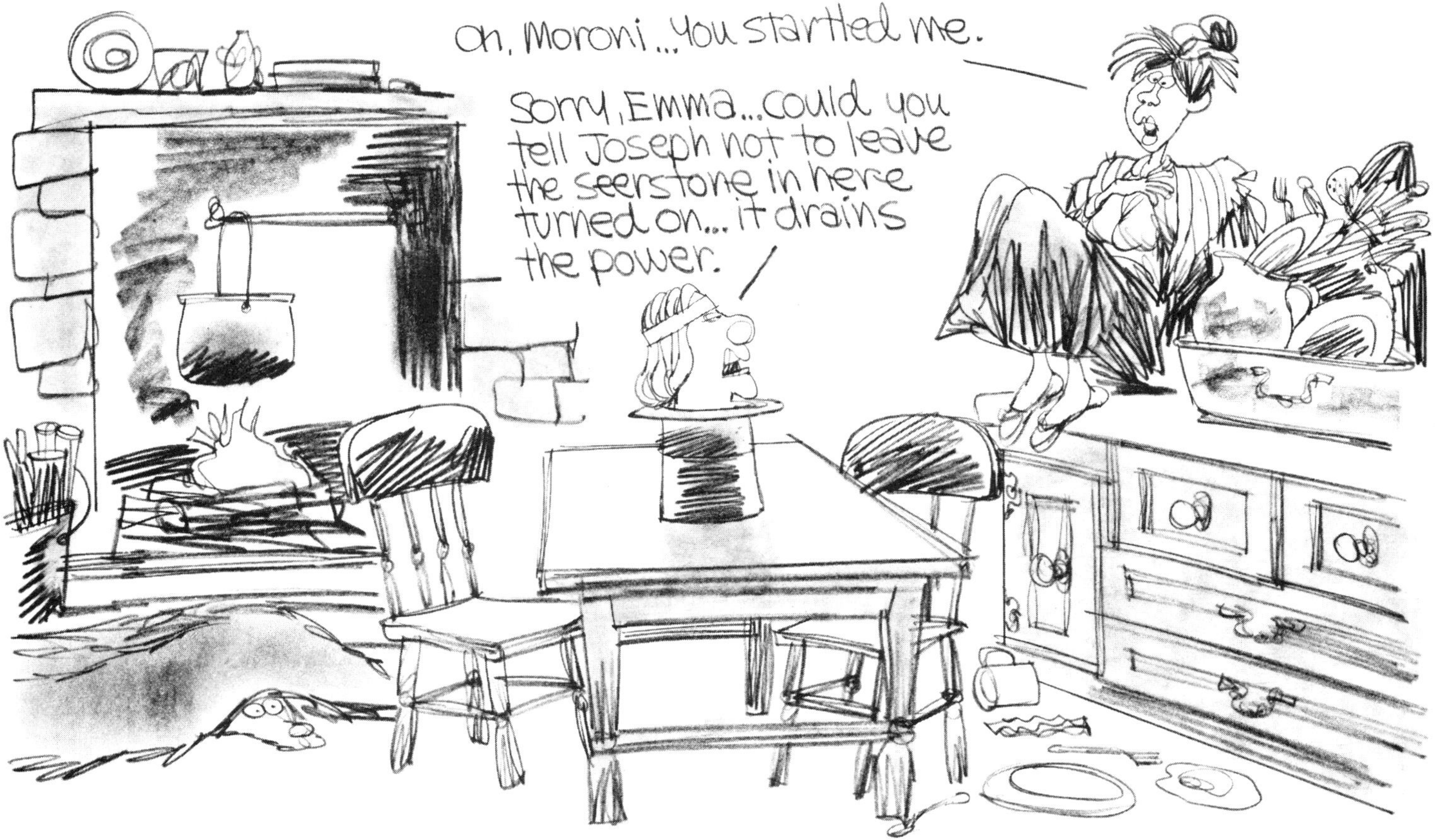
Oh, Moroni... You startled me.
Sorry, Emma... could you tell Joseph not to leave the seerstone in here turned on... it drains the power.

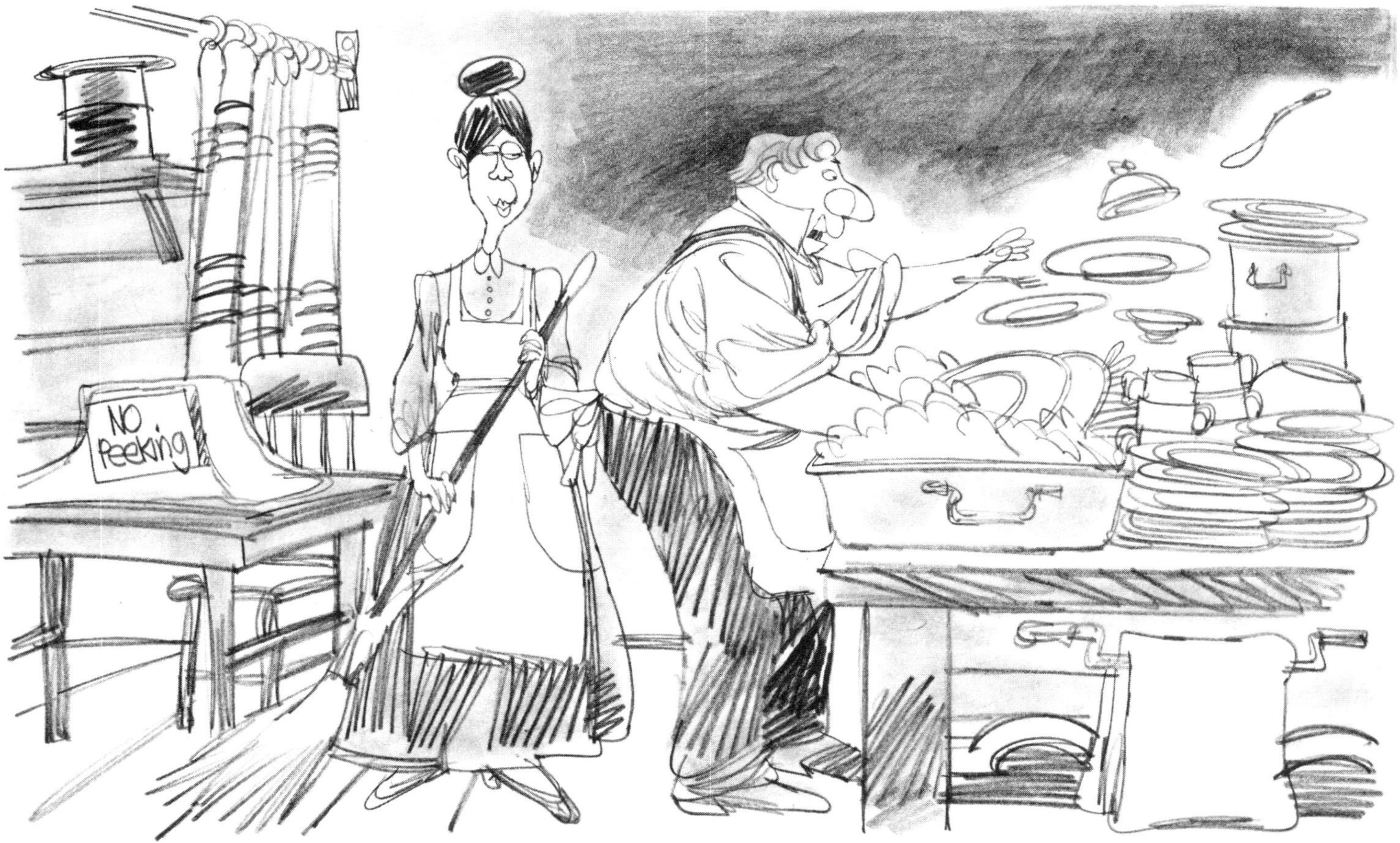
NO
Peeking

"Translate the plates. Wash the plates. Translate the plates. Wash the plates.
Where's Oliver? He was supposed to dry."

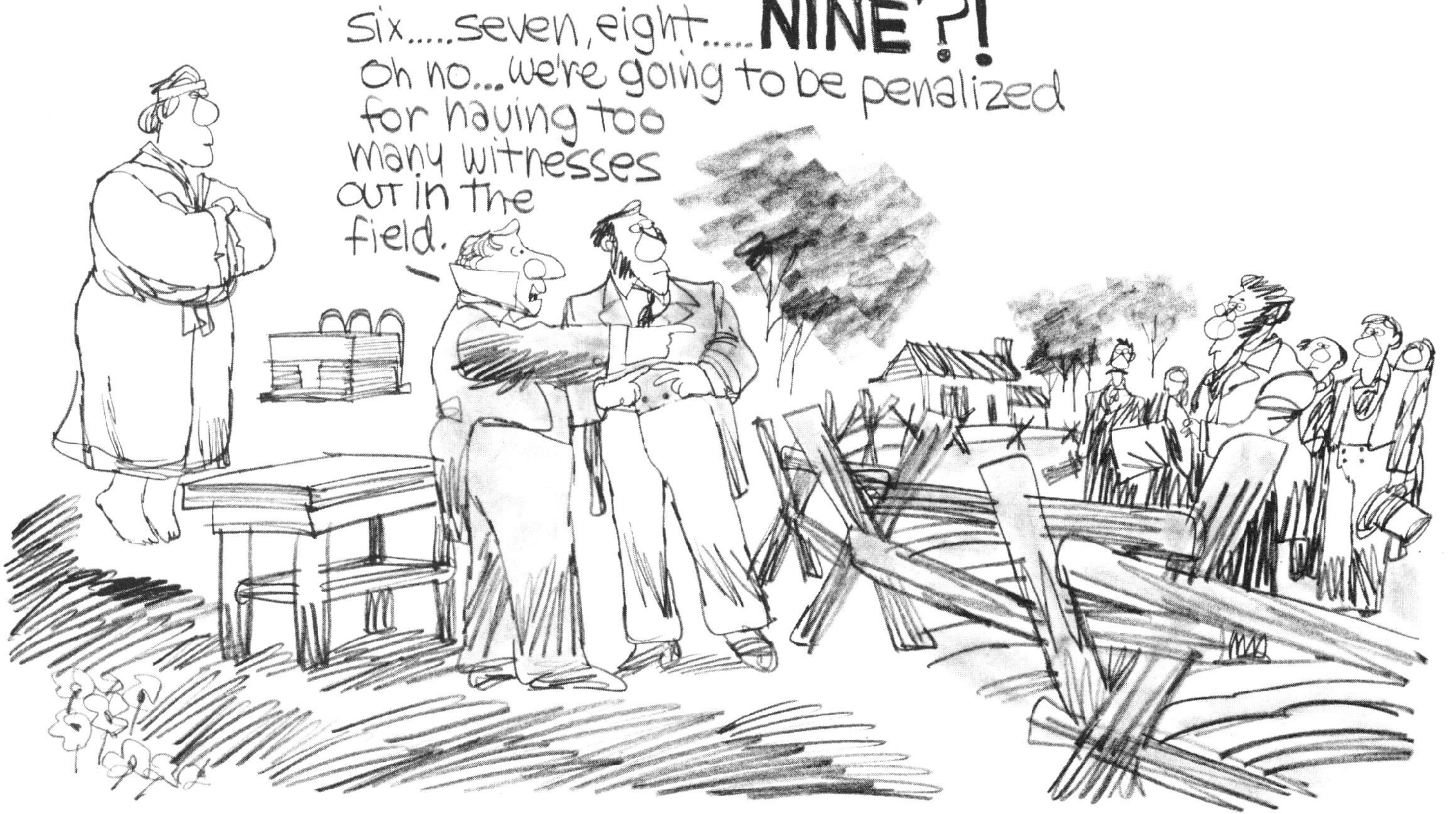
six.....seven, eight.....NINE?!
Oh no...we're going to be penalized for having too many witnesses out in the field.

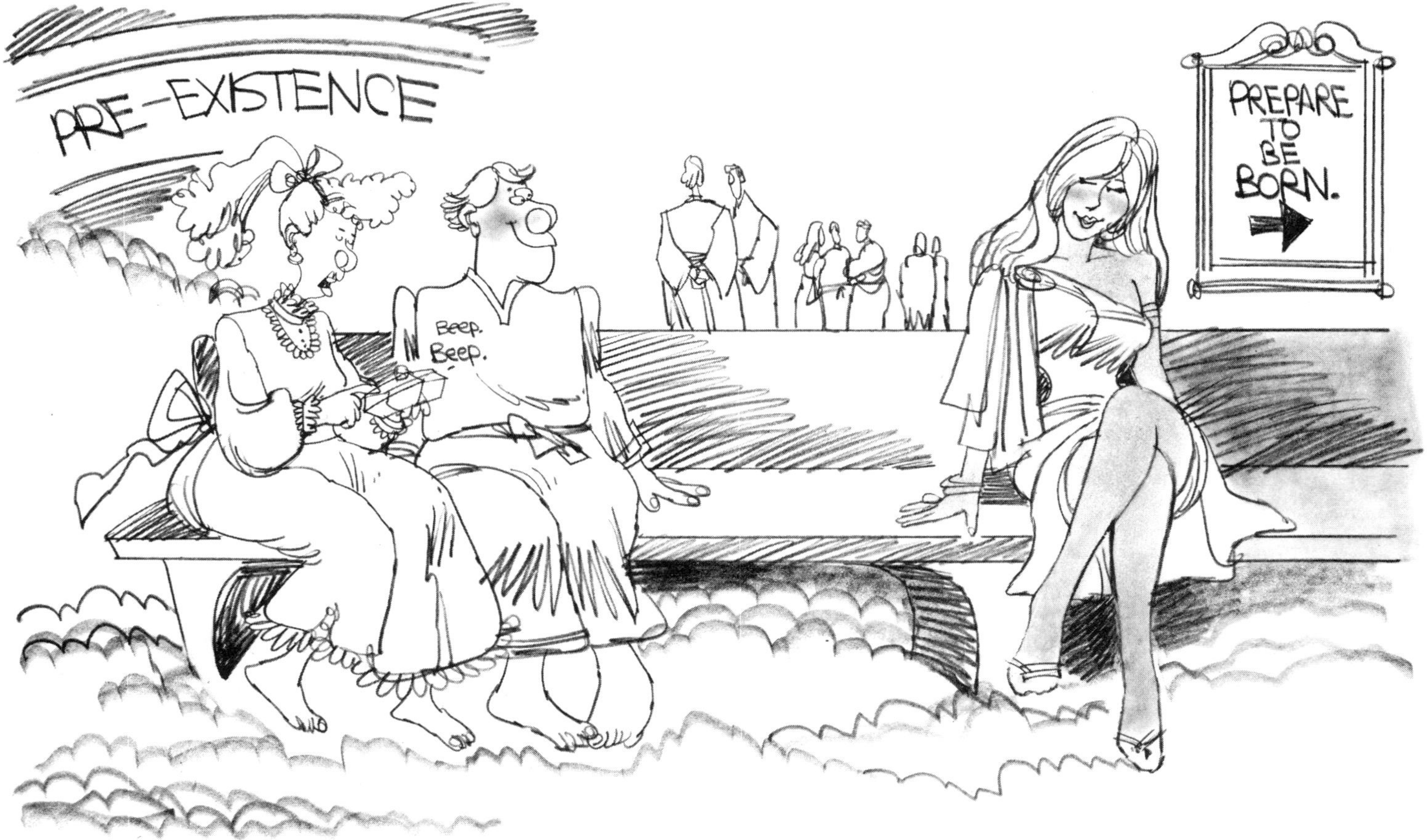
PRE-EXISTENCE
Beep.
Beep.
PREPARE
TO
BE
BORN.

"So, it's settled . . . After we're born we'll meet, fall in love, and marry in the temple.
Do you remember our meeting coordinates?"

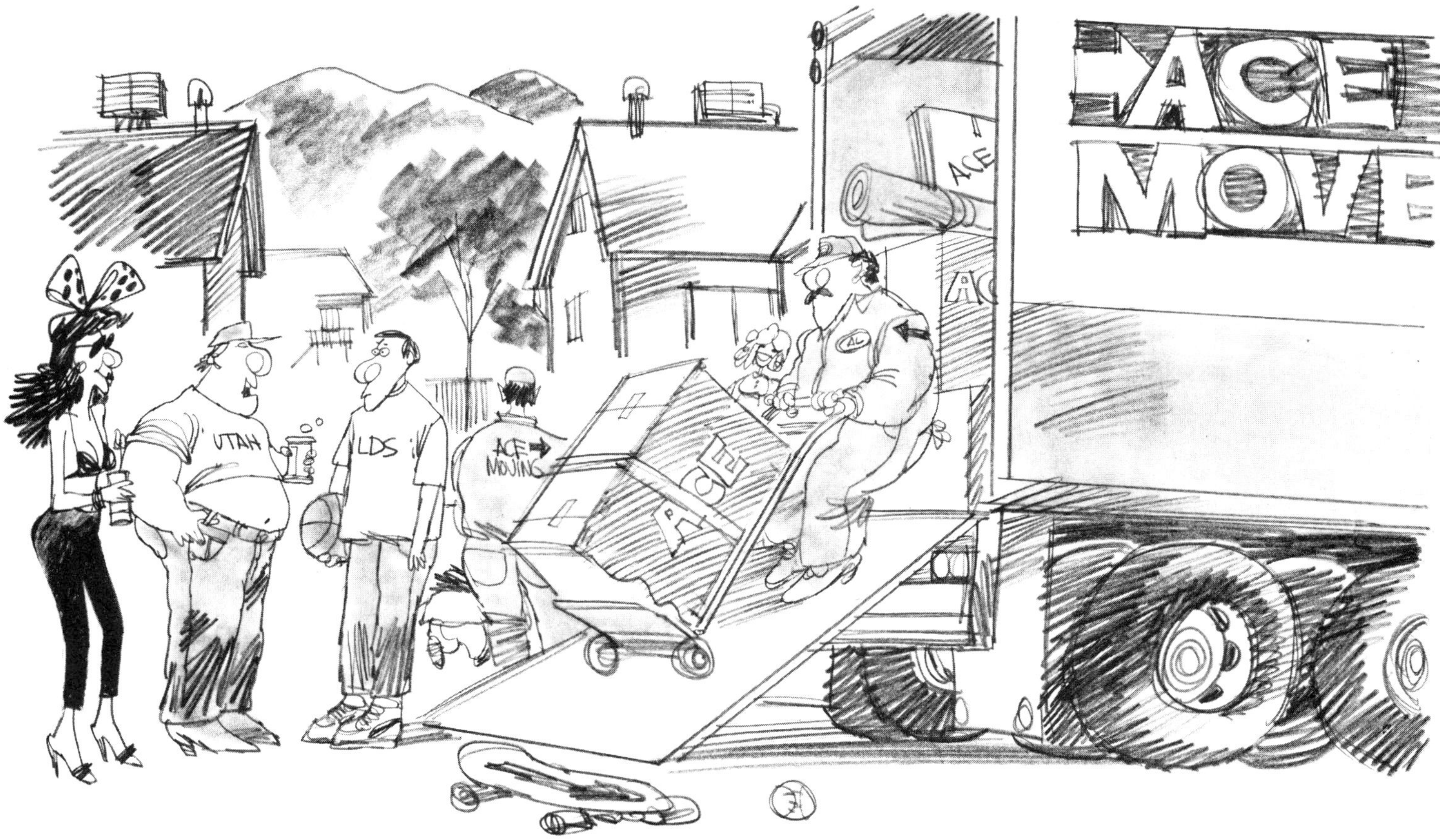
ACE
MOVE
UTAH
LDS
ACE
MOVING
ACE

"Welcome to Utah. How much do you know about Mormons who *don't* go to church? Would you like to know more?"

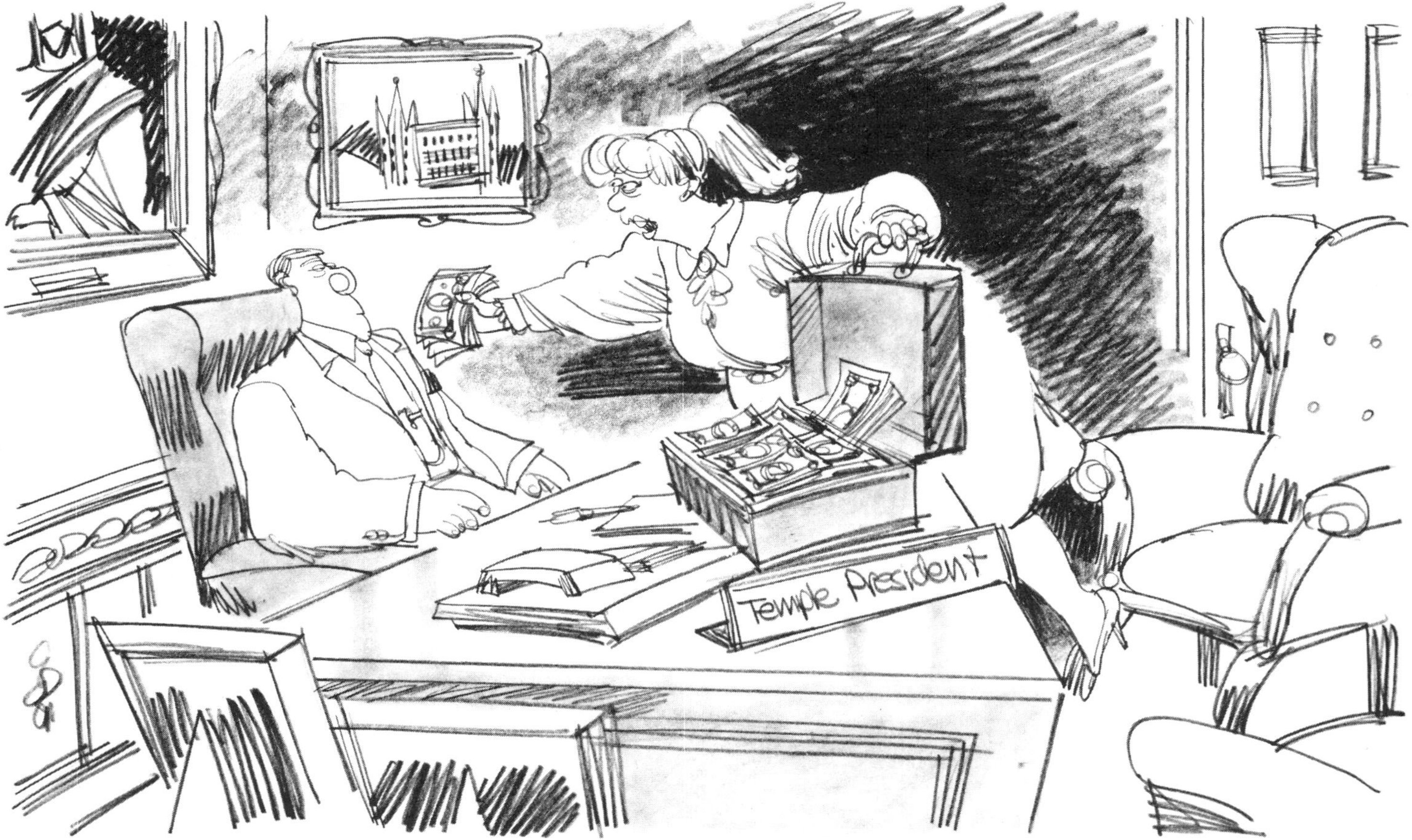
Temple President

"Here! Seal me to Elvis Presley!"

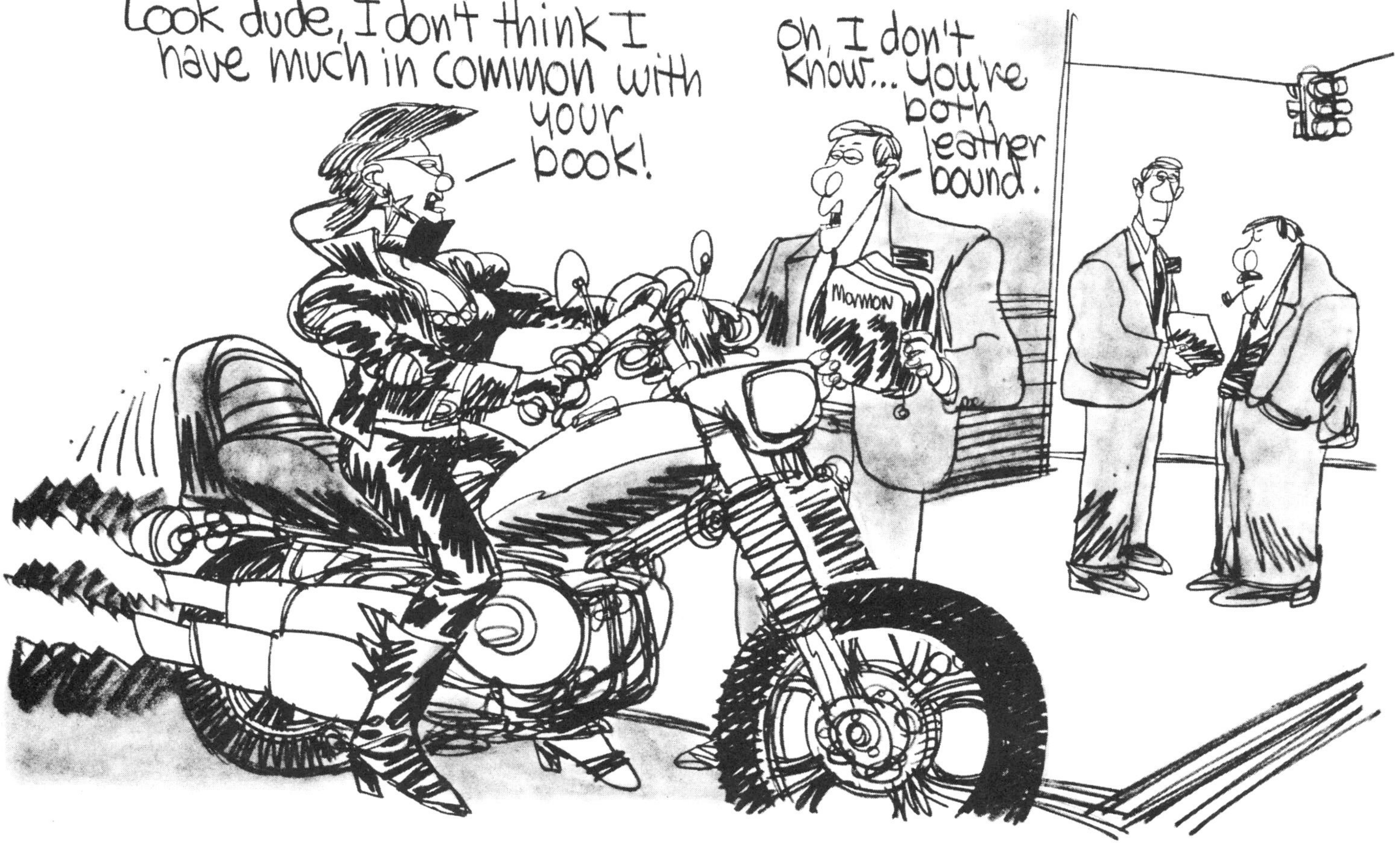
Look dude, I don't think I have much in common with your book!
Oh, I don't know... You're both leather bound.
Mormon

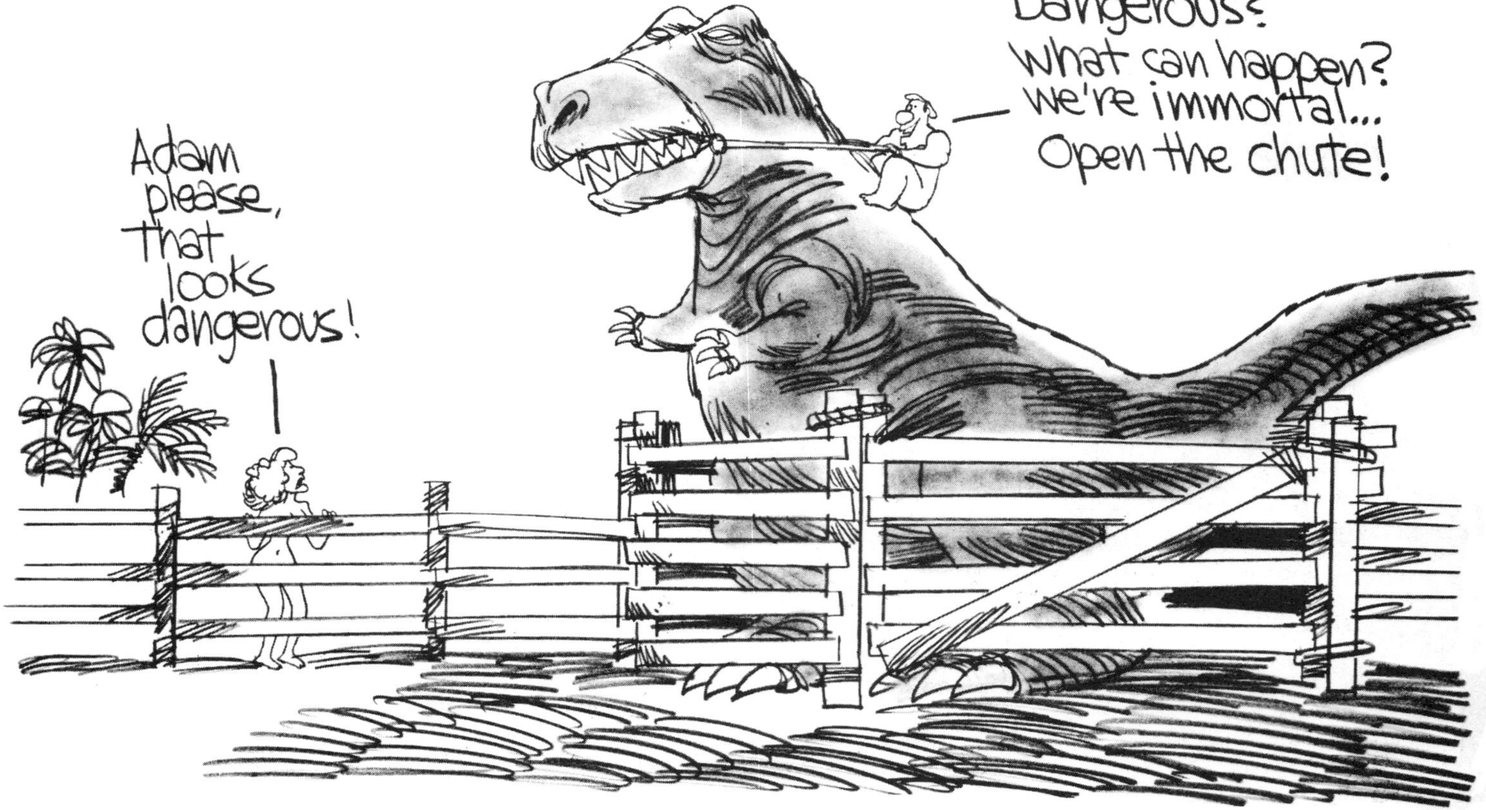
Adam please, That looks dangerous!
Dangerous? What can happen? We're immortal... Open the chute!

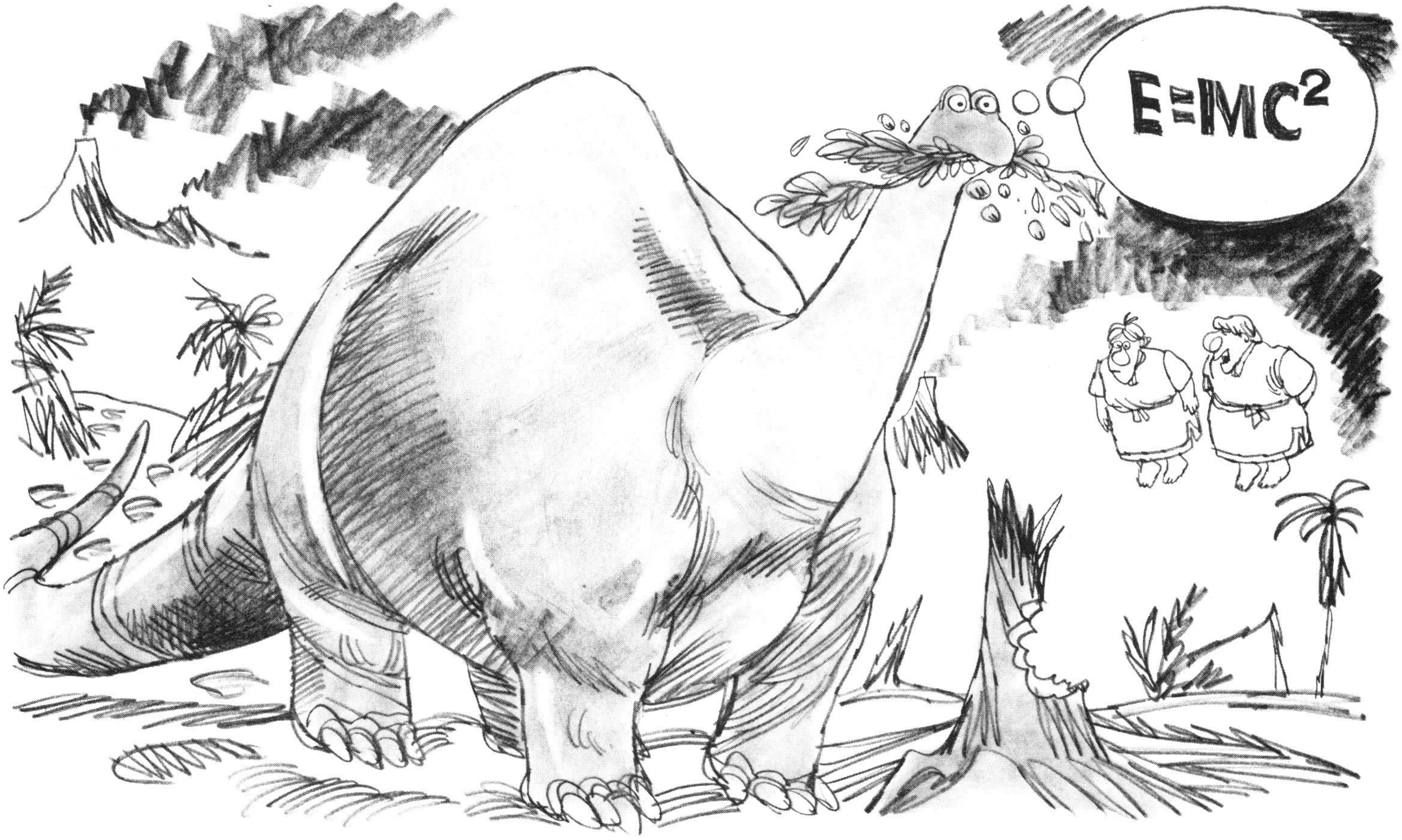
E=MC²

"I thought I told you to stand guard over the Tree of Knowledge."

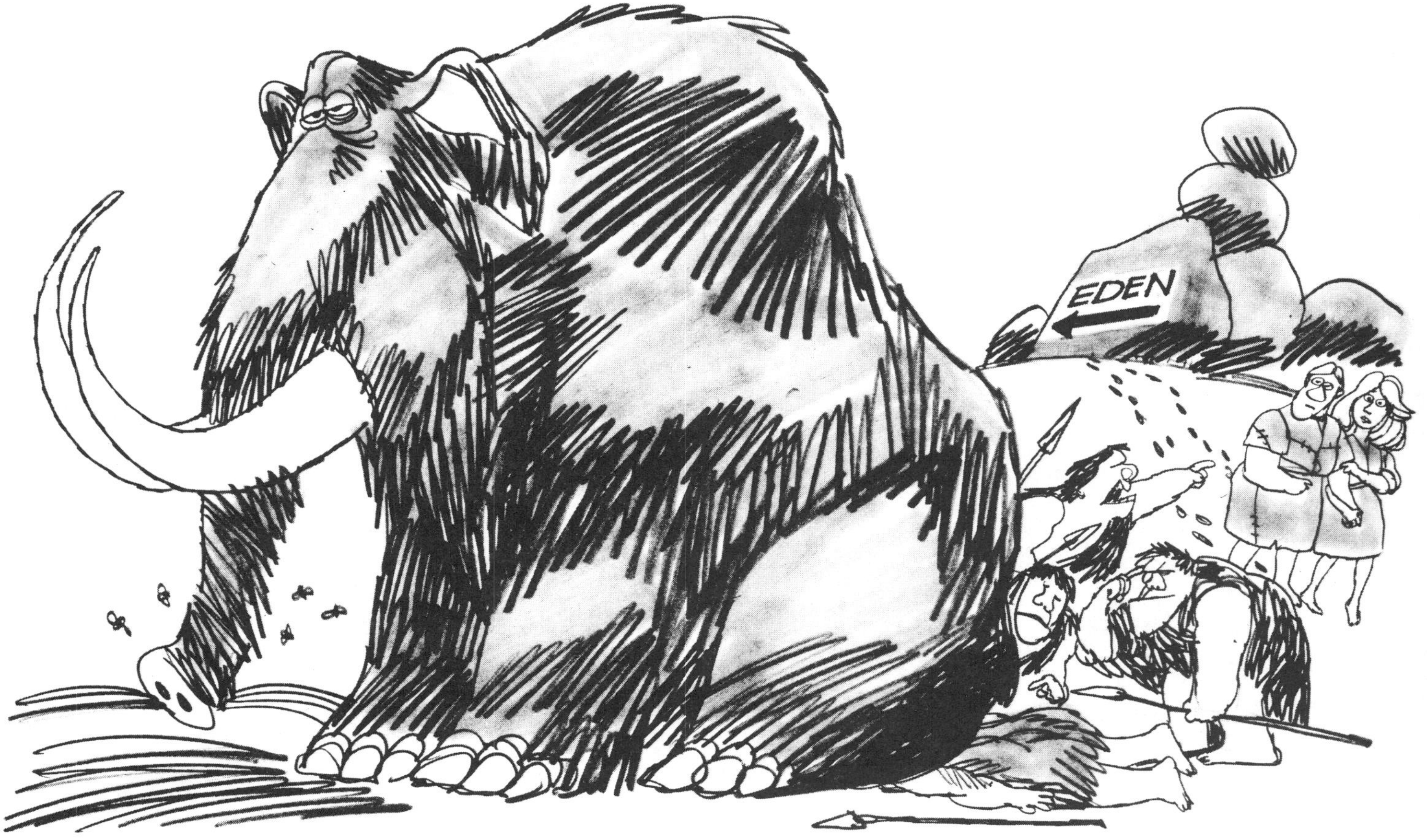
EDEN

"This is all your fault! If you hadn't brought death into the world . . ."

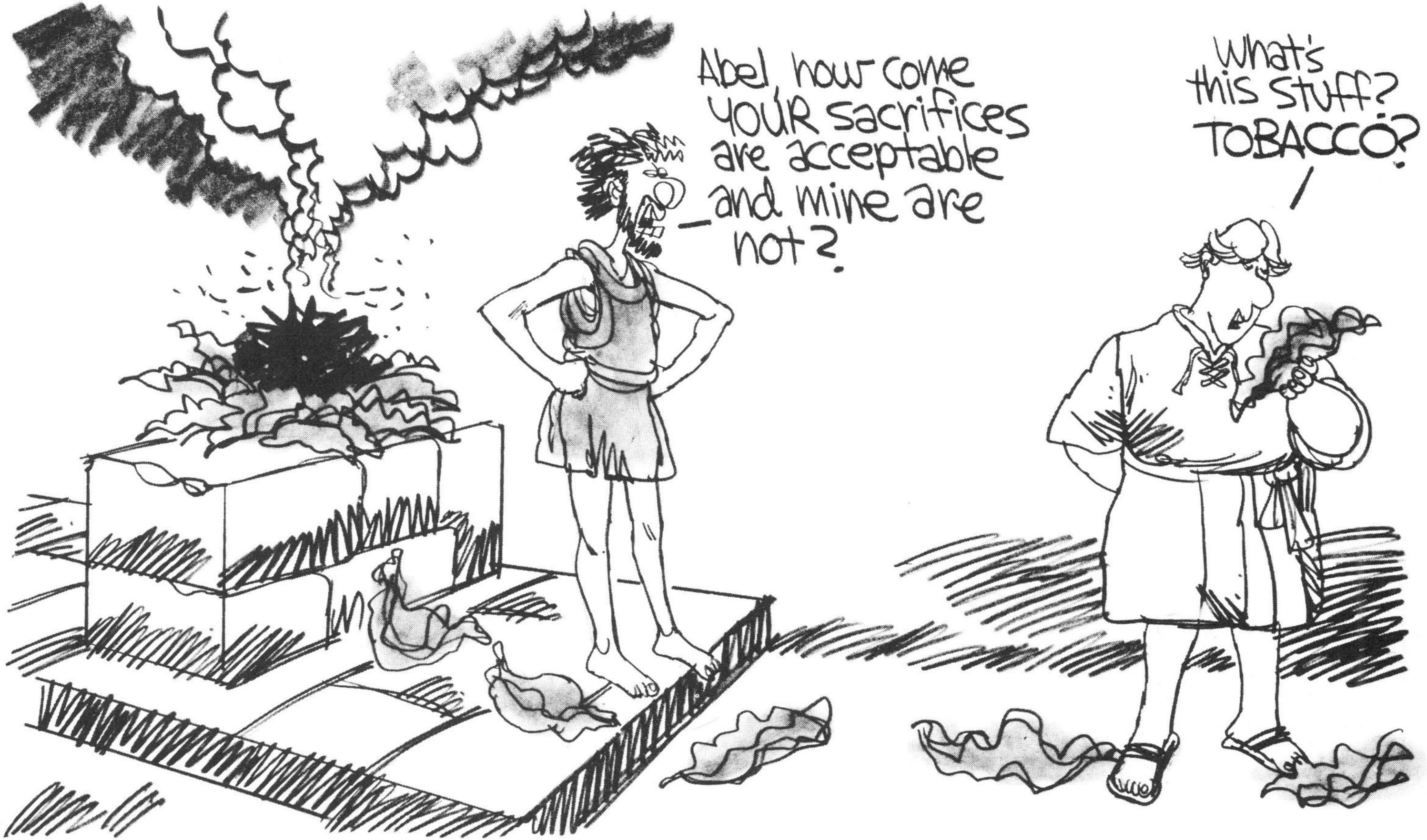
Abel how come YOUR sacrifices are acceptable and mine are not?
What's this stuff? TOBACCO?

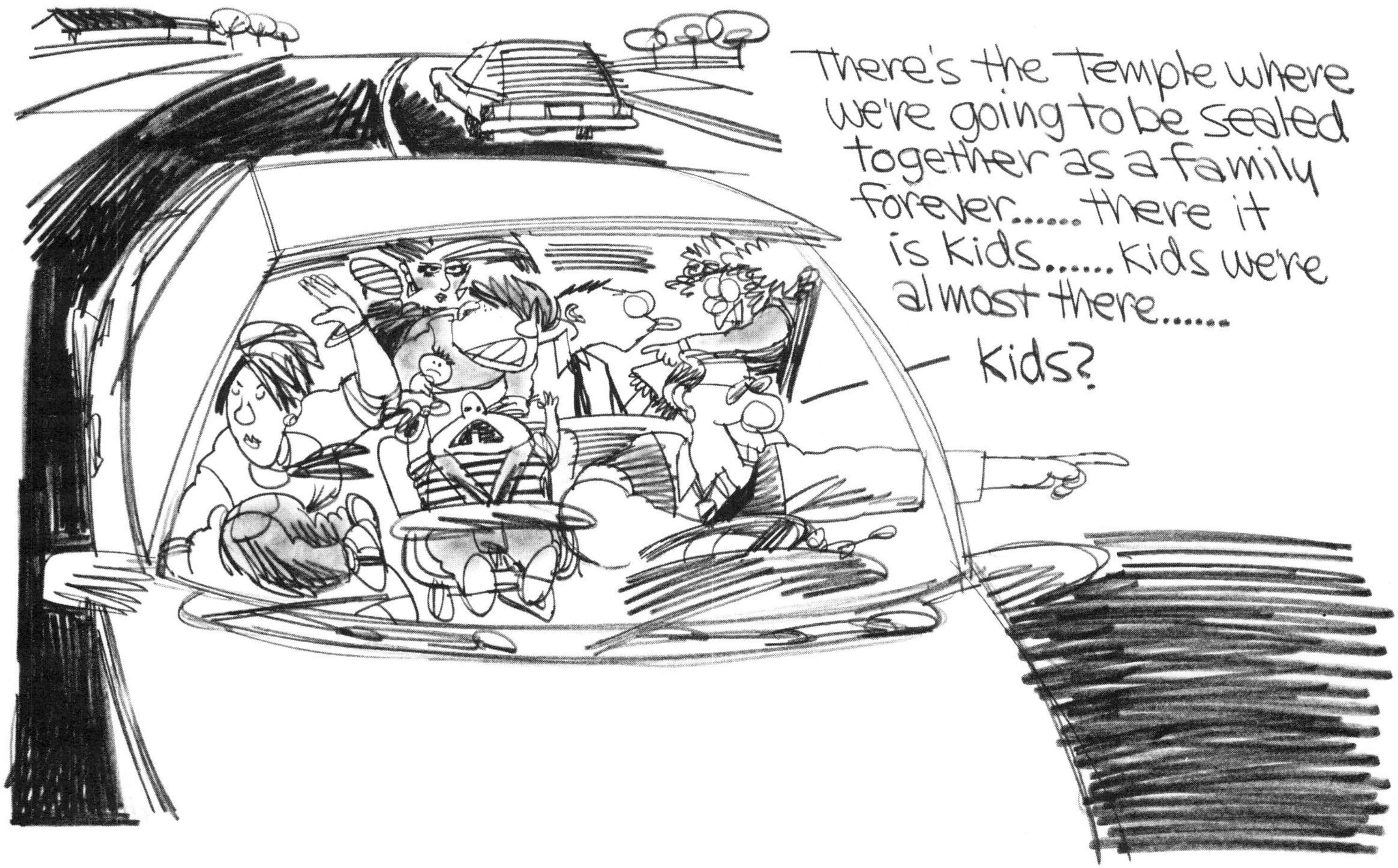
There's the Temple where we're going to be sealed together as a family forever...... there it is kids...... kids we're almost there......
kids?

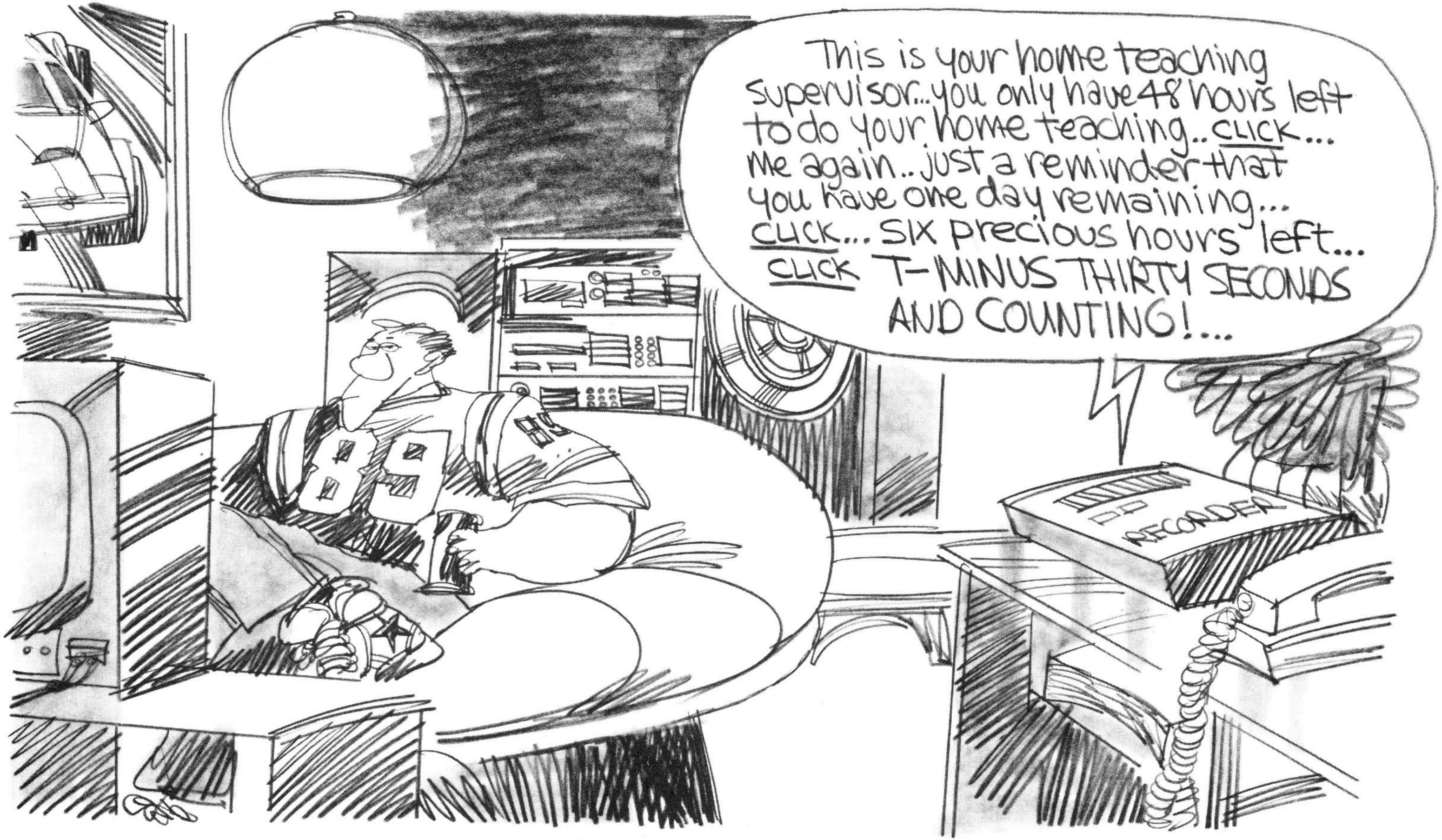
This is your home teaching supervisor...you only have 48 hours left to do your home teaching...CLICK... me again...just a reminder that you have one day remaining... CLICK... SIX precious hours left... CLICK T-MINUS THIRTY SECONDS AND COUNTING!...
89
RECORDER

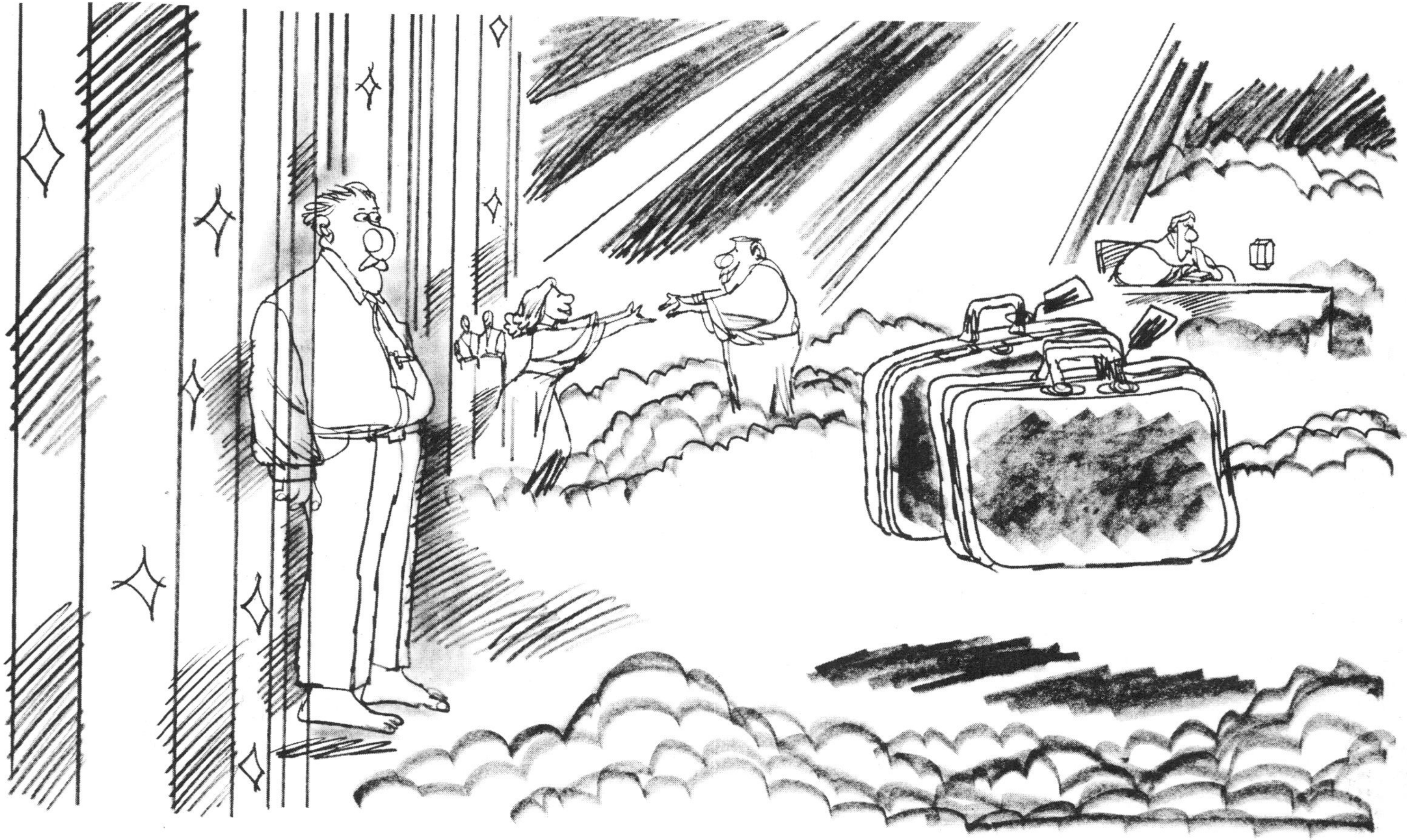

Harold dies and is met at the veil by his luggage . . . lost and never recovered by the airline ten years ago.

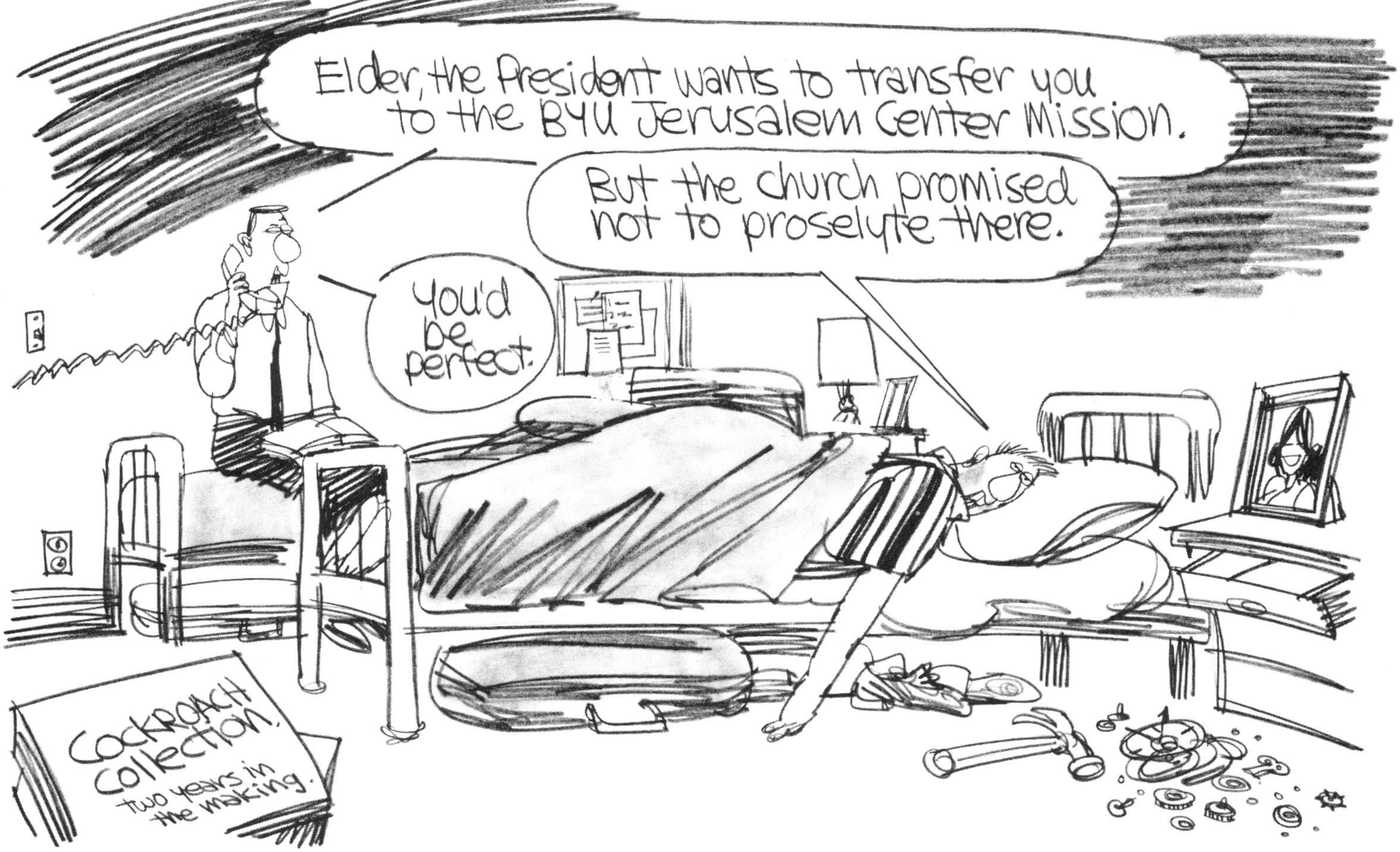
Elder, the President wants to transfer you to the BYU Jerusalem Center Mission.
You'd be perfect.
But the church promised not to proselyte there.
COCKROACH Collection. two years in the making.

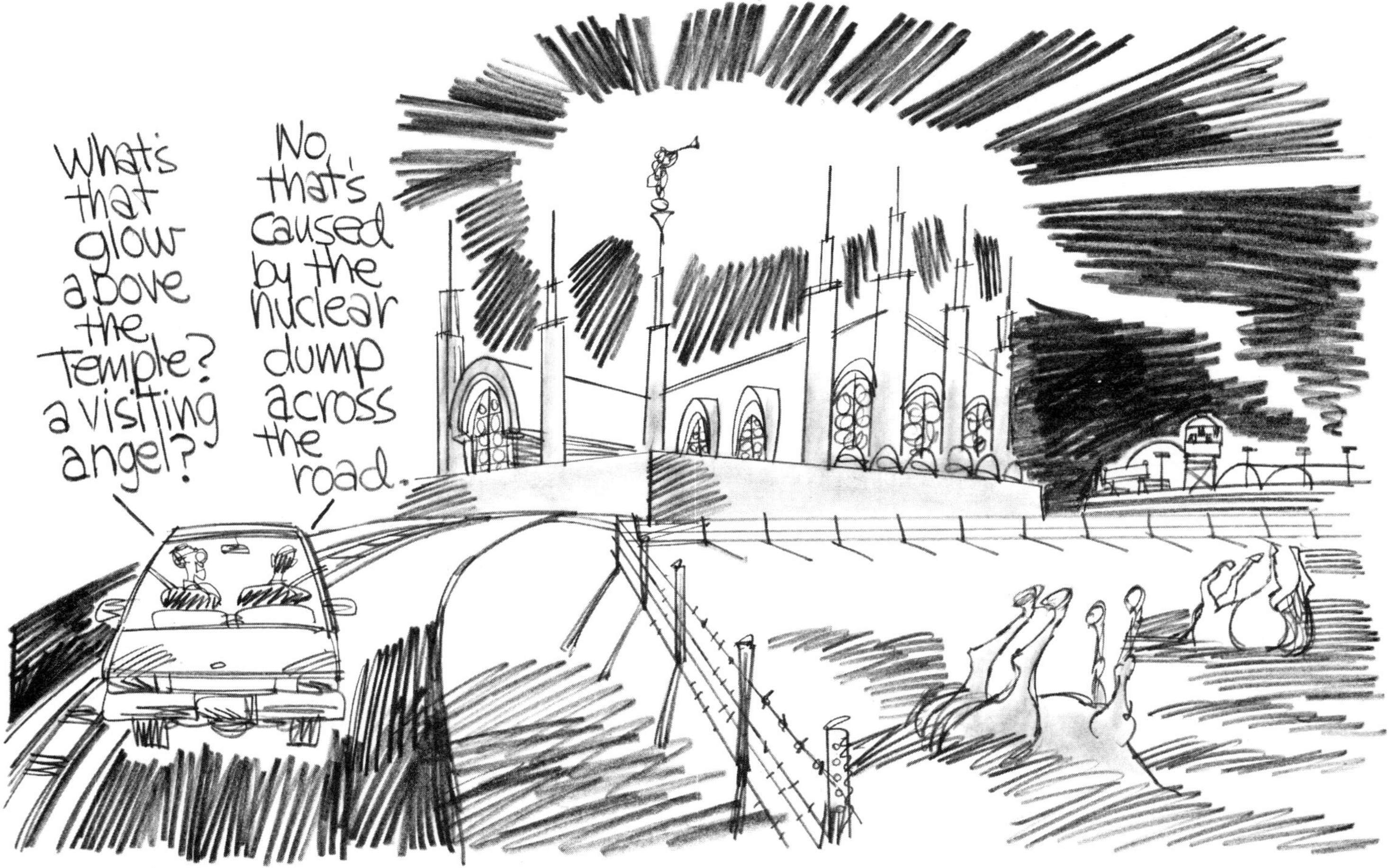
What's that glow above the Temple? a visiting angel?
No, that's caused by the nuclear dump across the road.

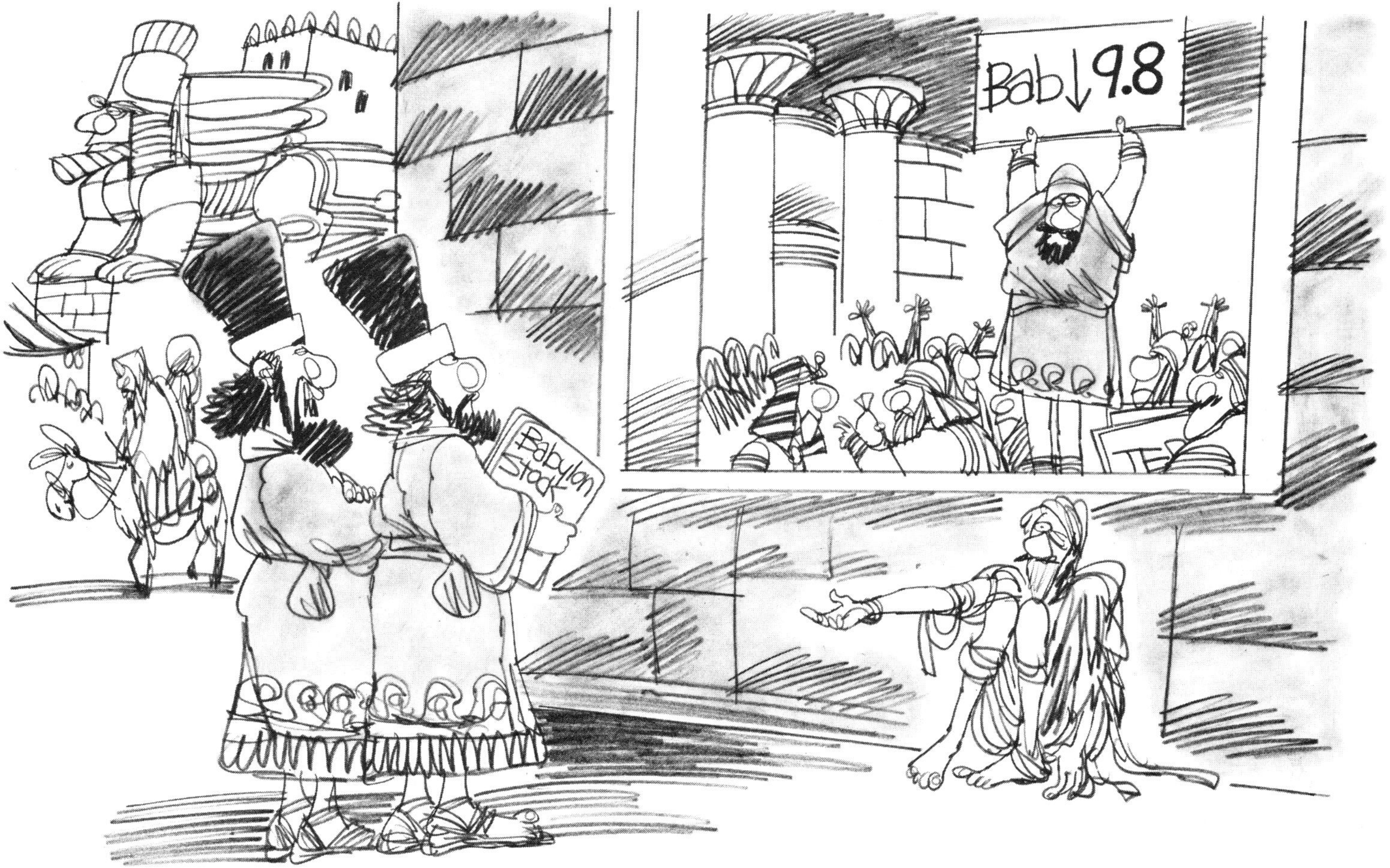
Bab↓9.8
Babylon Stock

"Better sell. It looks like Babylon the Great is falling."

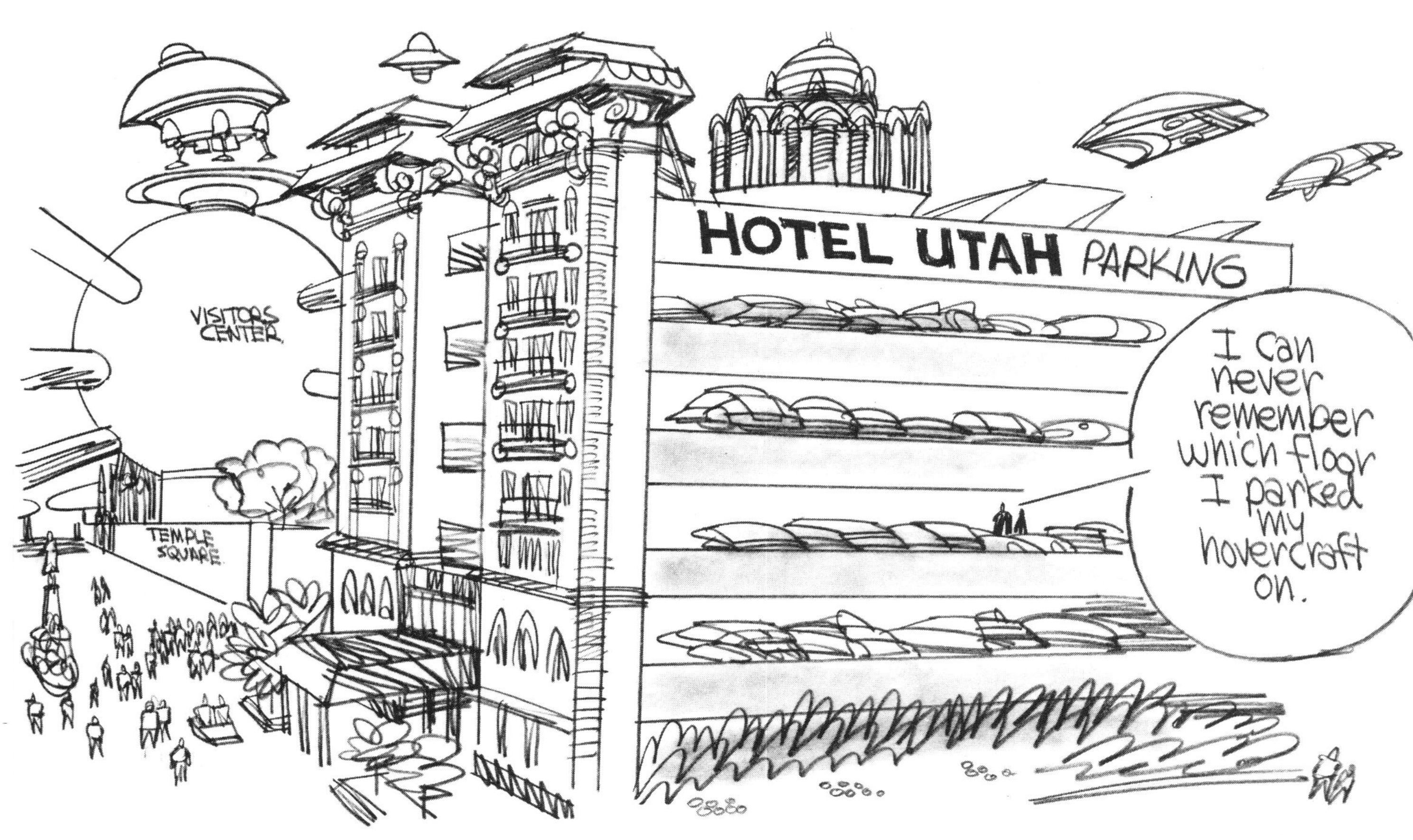
VISITORS CENTER
HOTEL UTAH PARKING
TEMPLE SQUARE
I can never remember which floor I parked my hovercraft on.

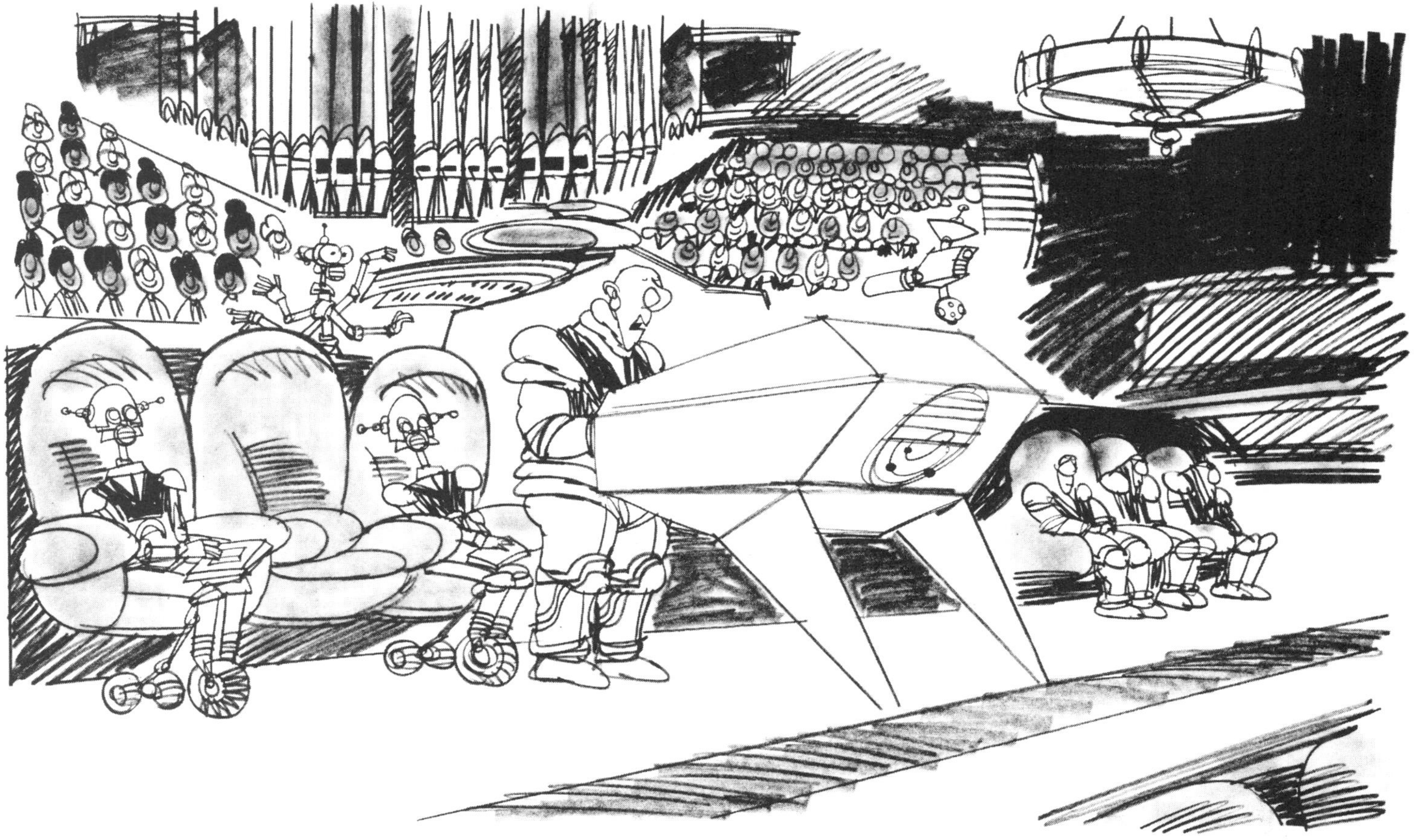

“And a special thanks for my two new counselors. Without their superhuman effort I could not preside over this church with its hundreds of millions of members.”

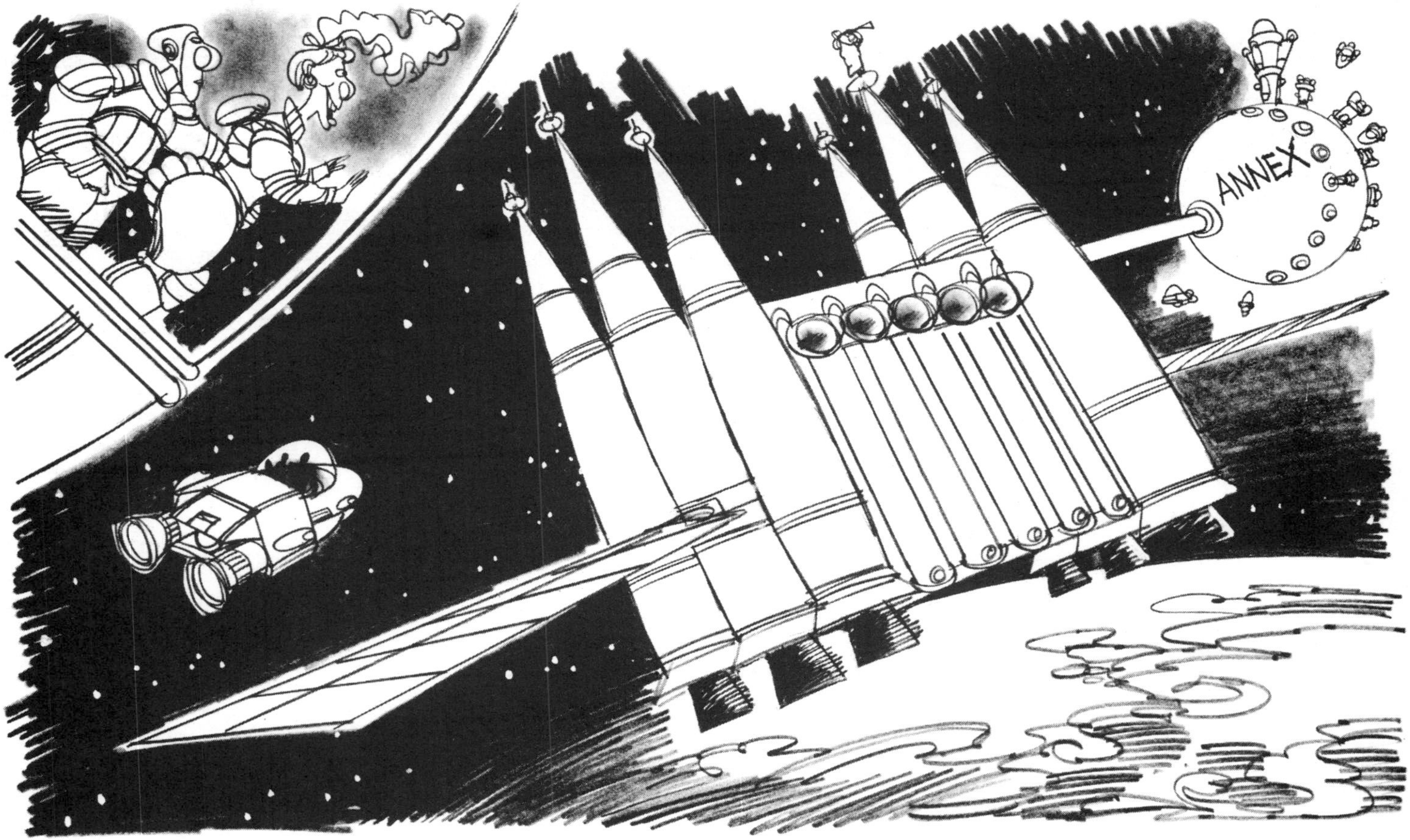
ANNEX

“Don’t you just love the classic lines of our first orbiting temple?”

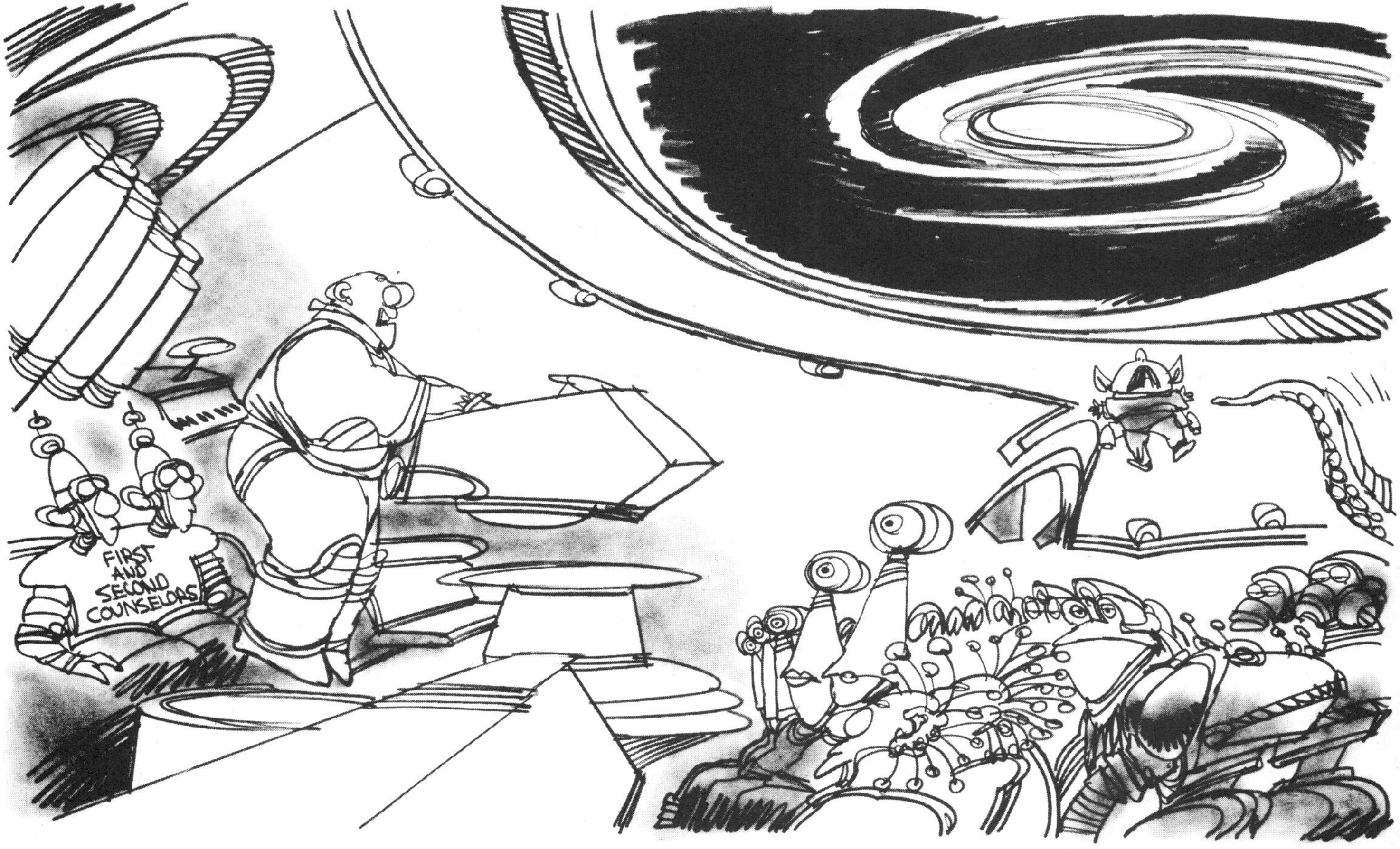
FIRST AND SECOND COUNSELORS

"A long time ago, in a galaxy far, far away, our church only had six members."

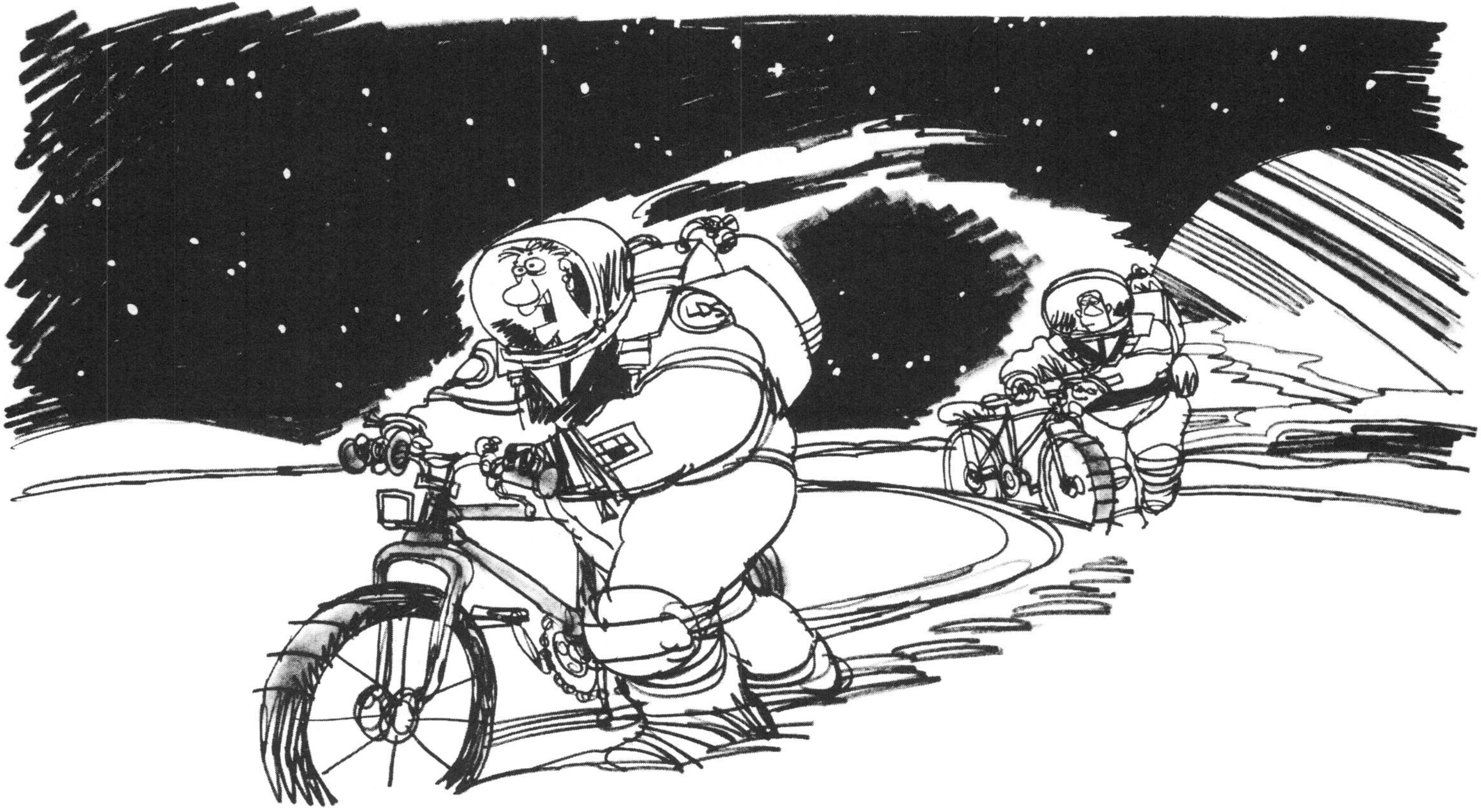
LDS

"His two-year mission: to seek out strange new converts, to boldly go where no missionary has gone before."

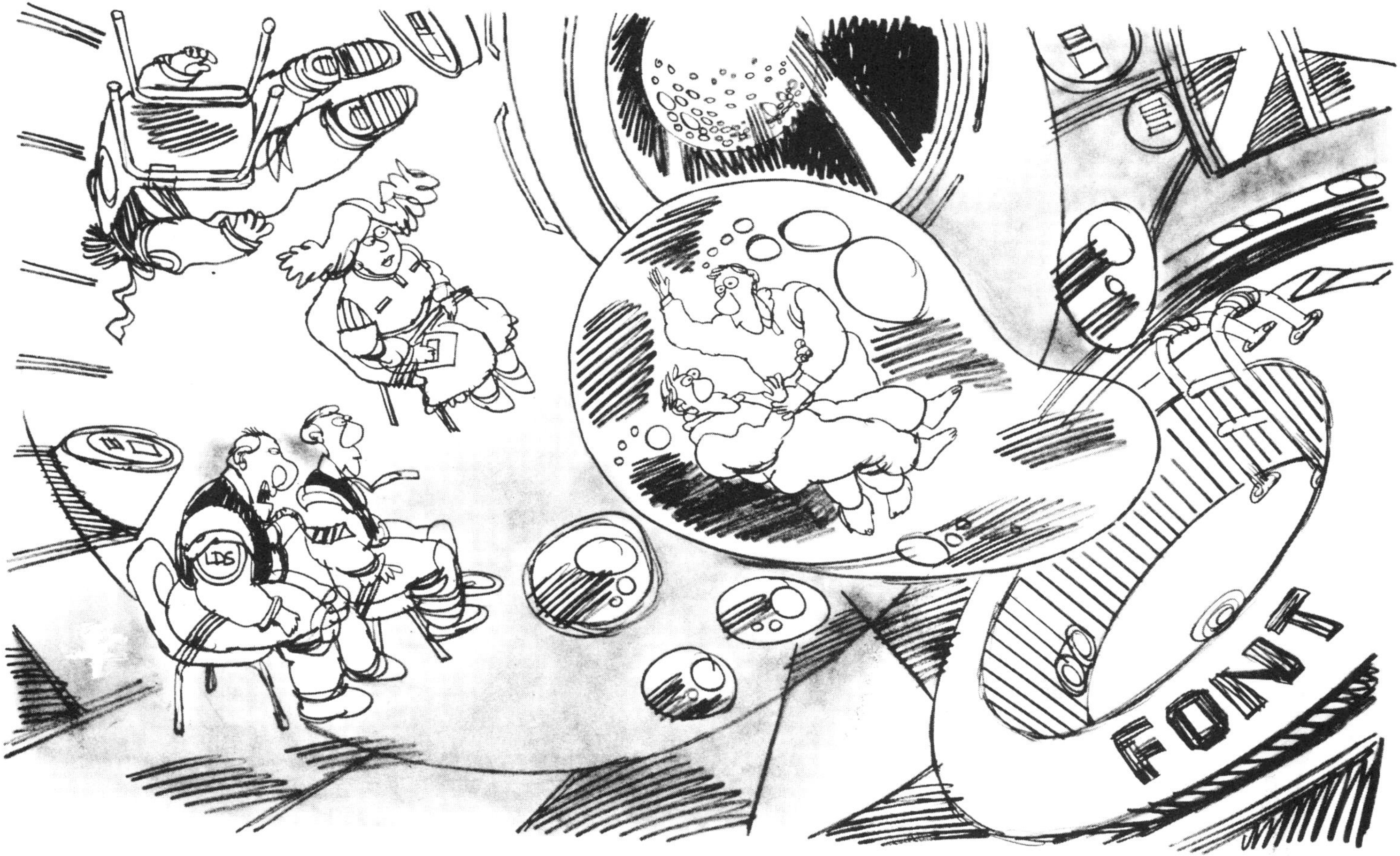
LDS
FONT

"Zero-gravity baptisms are always a bit tricky."

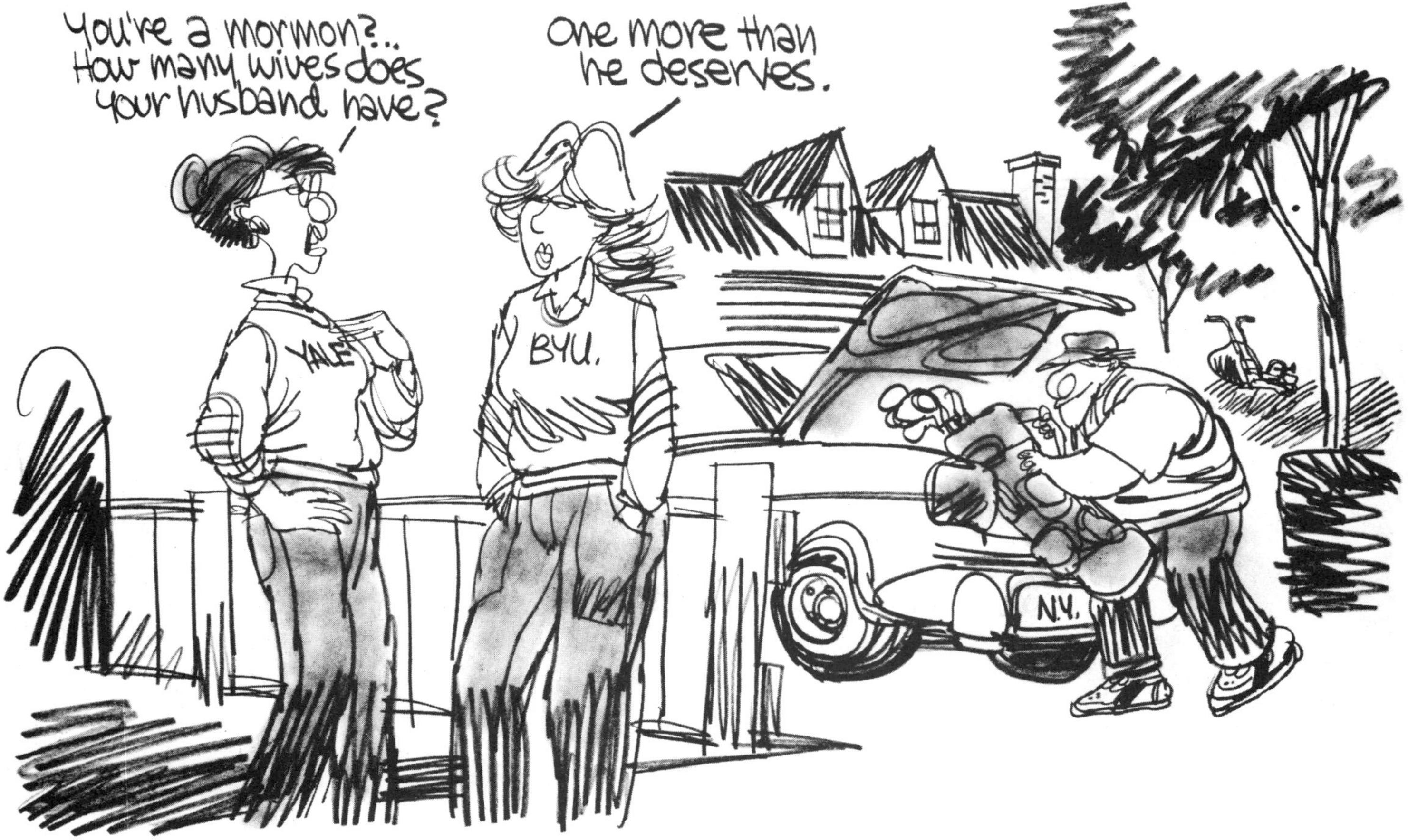
You're a mormon?...
How many wives does
your husband have?
One more than
he deserves.
YALE
BYU.
N.Y.

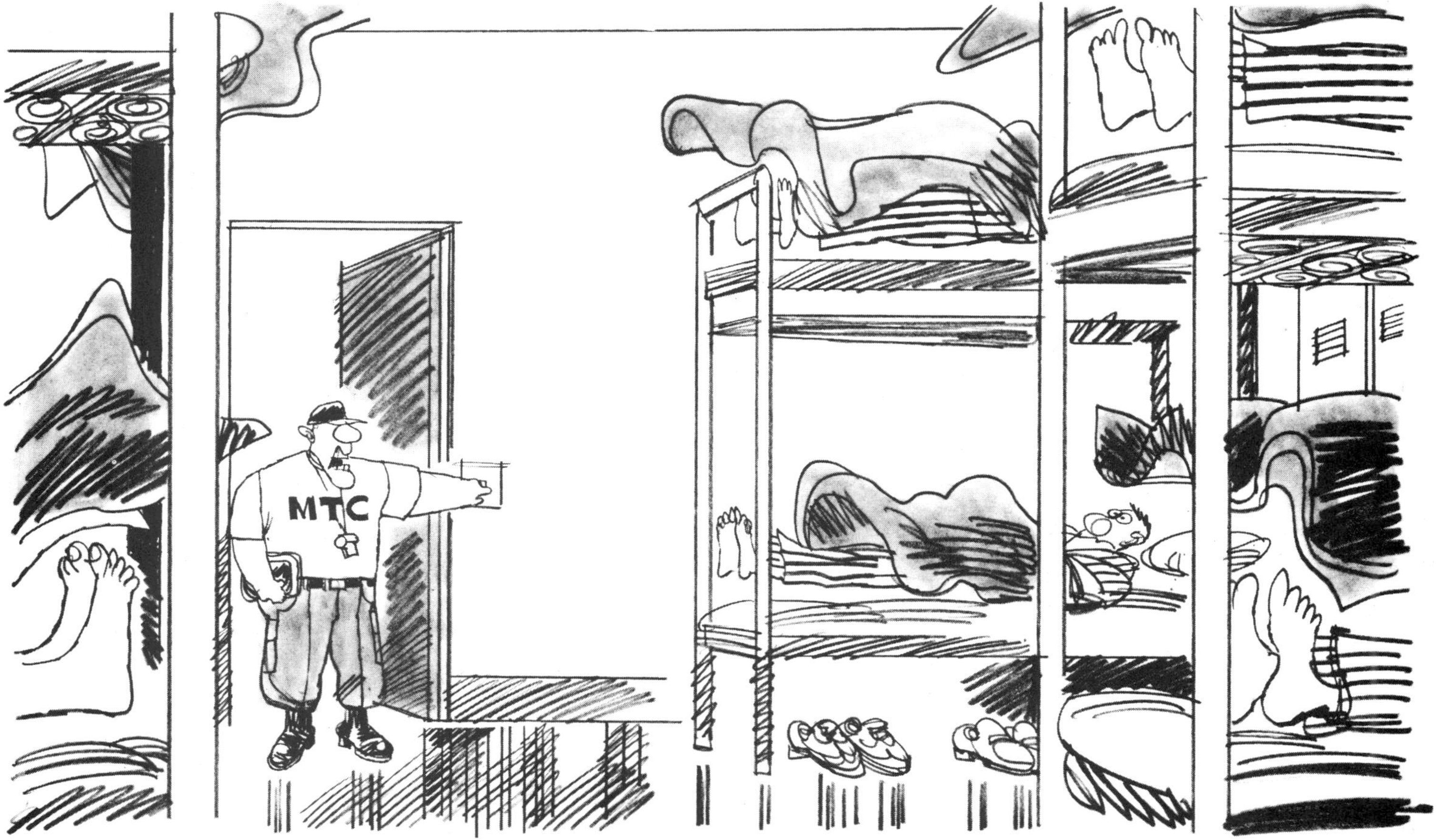
MTC

"Alright, get your feet down and your testimonies up."

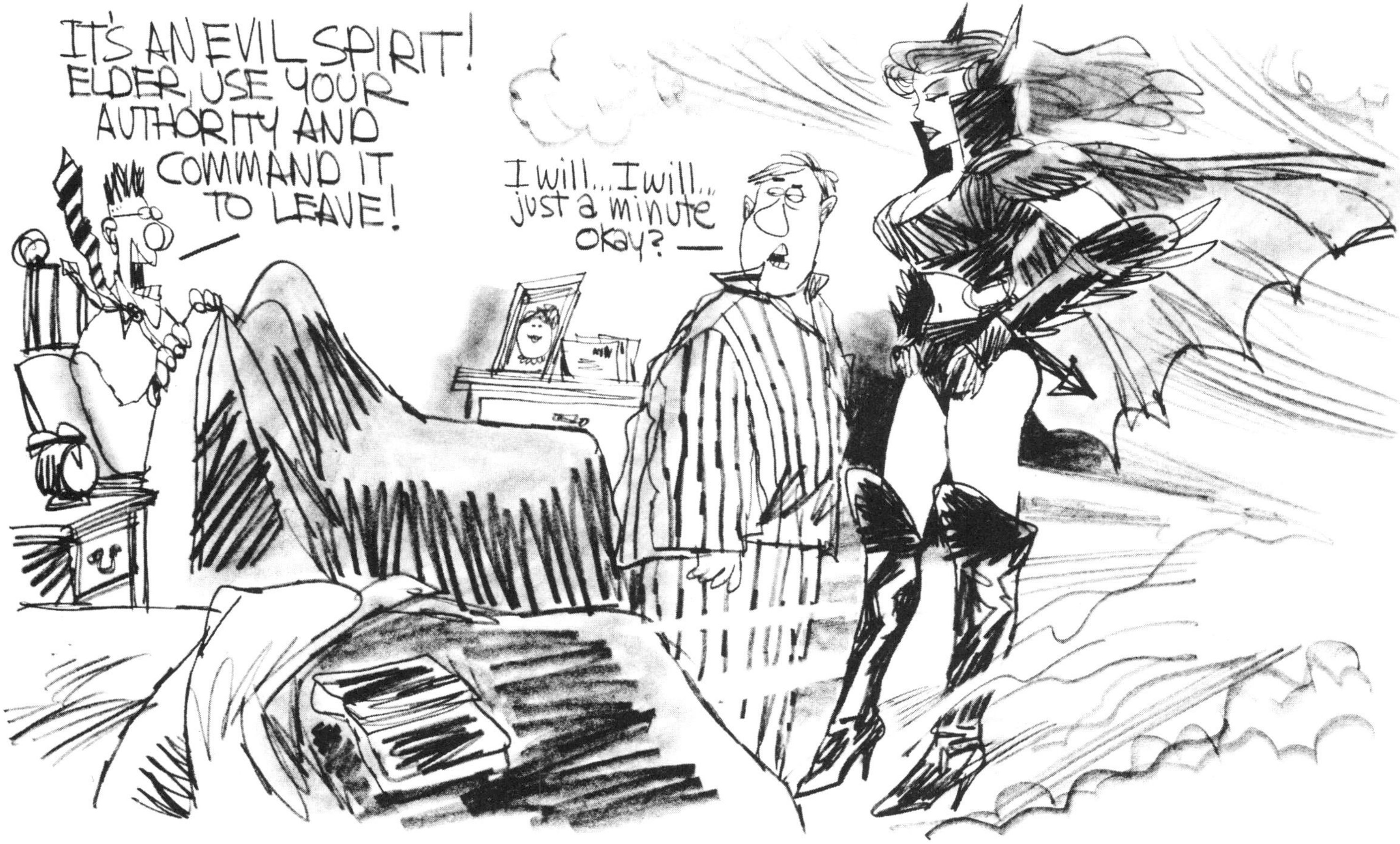
IT'S AN EVIL SPIRIT! ELDER, USE YOUR AUTHORITY AND COMMAND IT TO LEAVE!
I will... I will... just a minute okay?

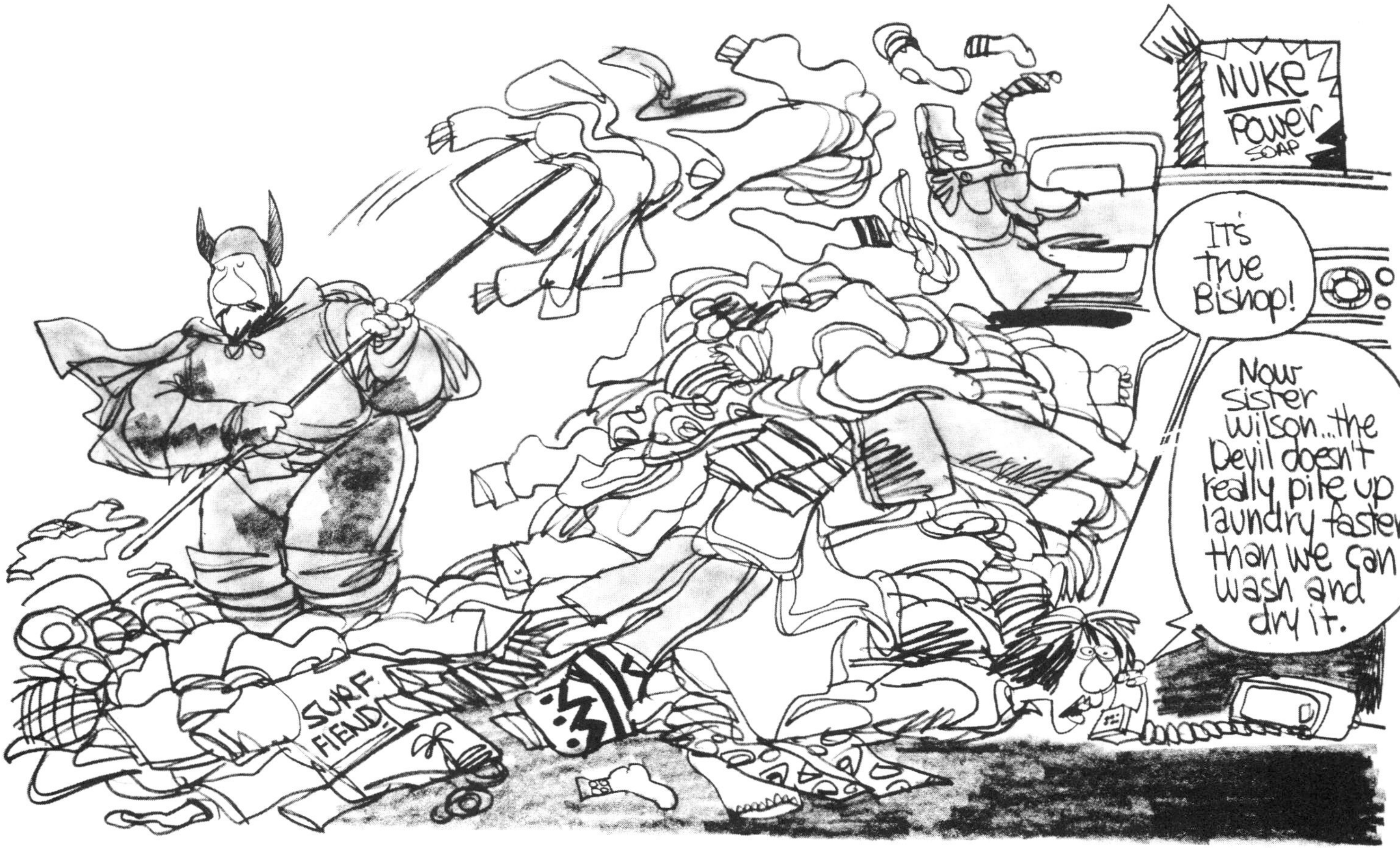
NUKE POWER SOAP
It's true Bishop!
Now sister Wilson...the Devil doesn't really pile up laundry faster than we can wash and dry it.
SURF FIEND

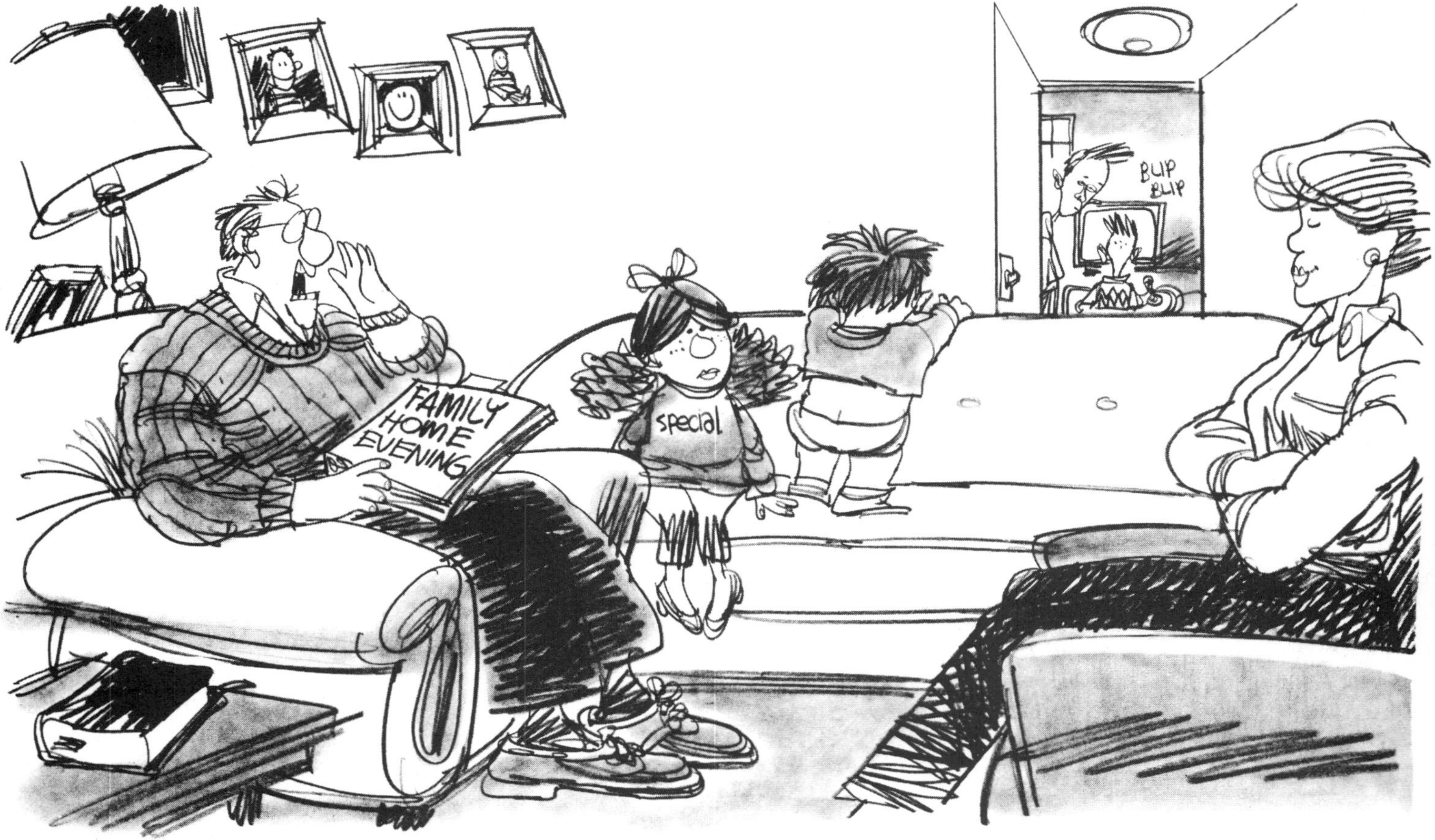

FAMILY HOME EVENING
Special
BLIP BLIP

"And other sheep I have which are not of this fold. They too shall hear my voice and COME THIS INSTANT!"

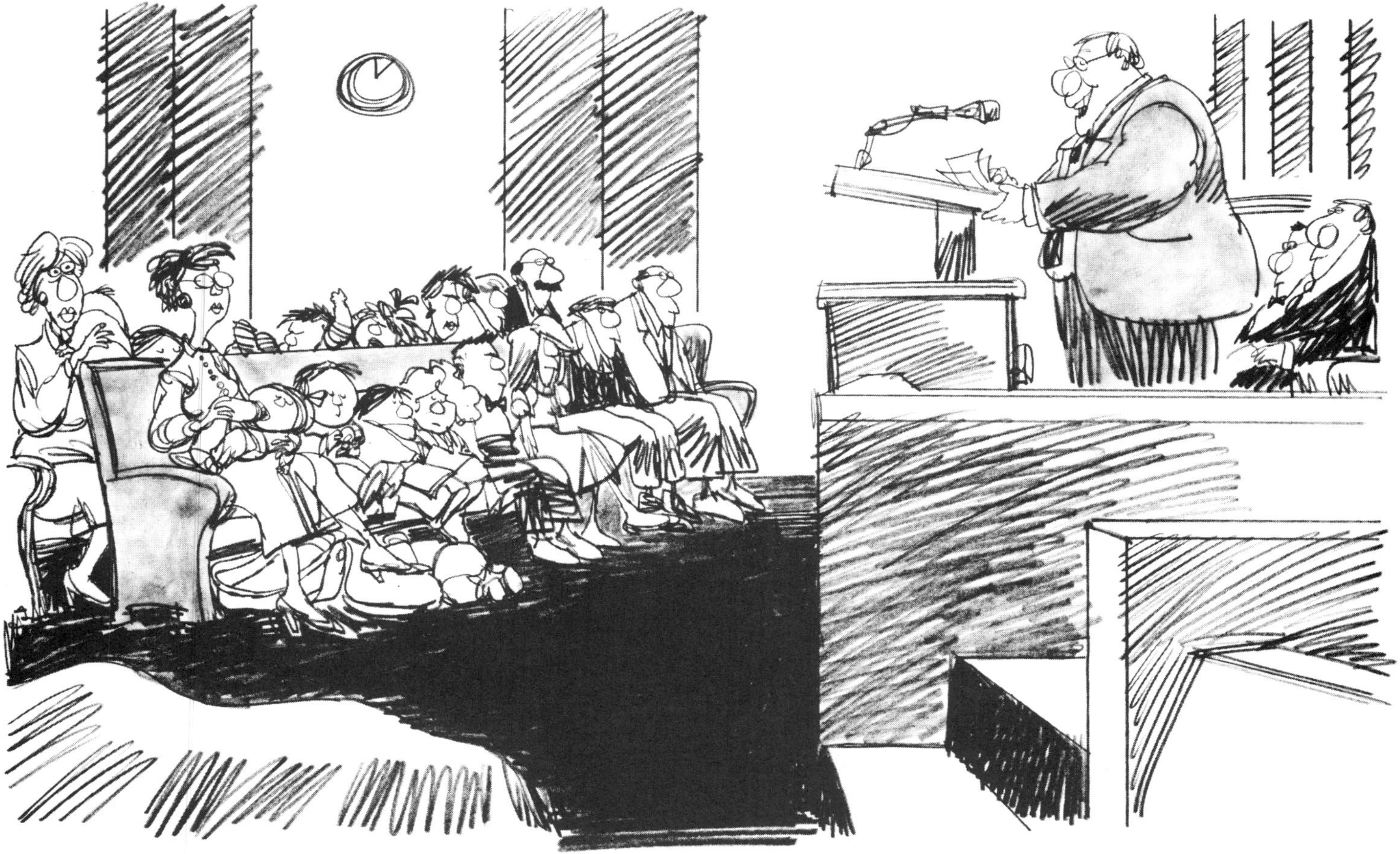

"Raising a family . . . brings a husband and wife closer together."

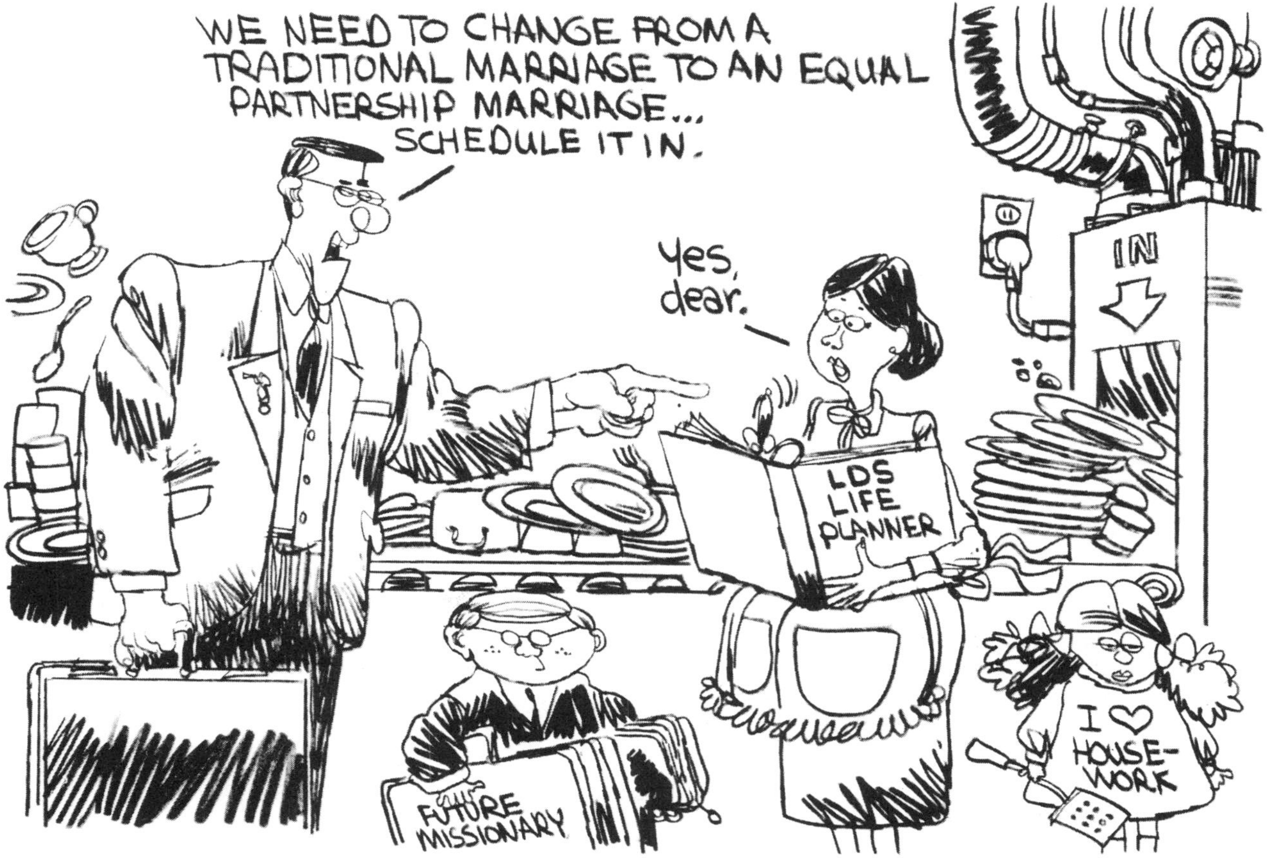
WE NEED TO CHANGE FROM A TRADITIONAL MARRIAGE TO AN EQUAL PARTNERSHIP MARRIAGE... SCHEDULE IT IN.
Yes, dear.
IN
LDS LIFE PLANNER
FUTURE MISSIONARY
I ♥ HOUSE-WORK

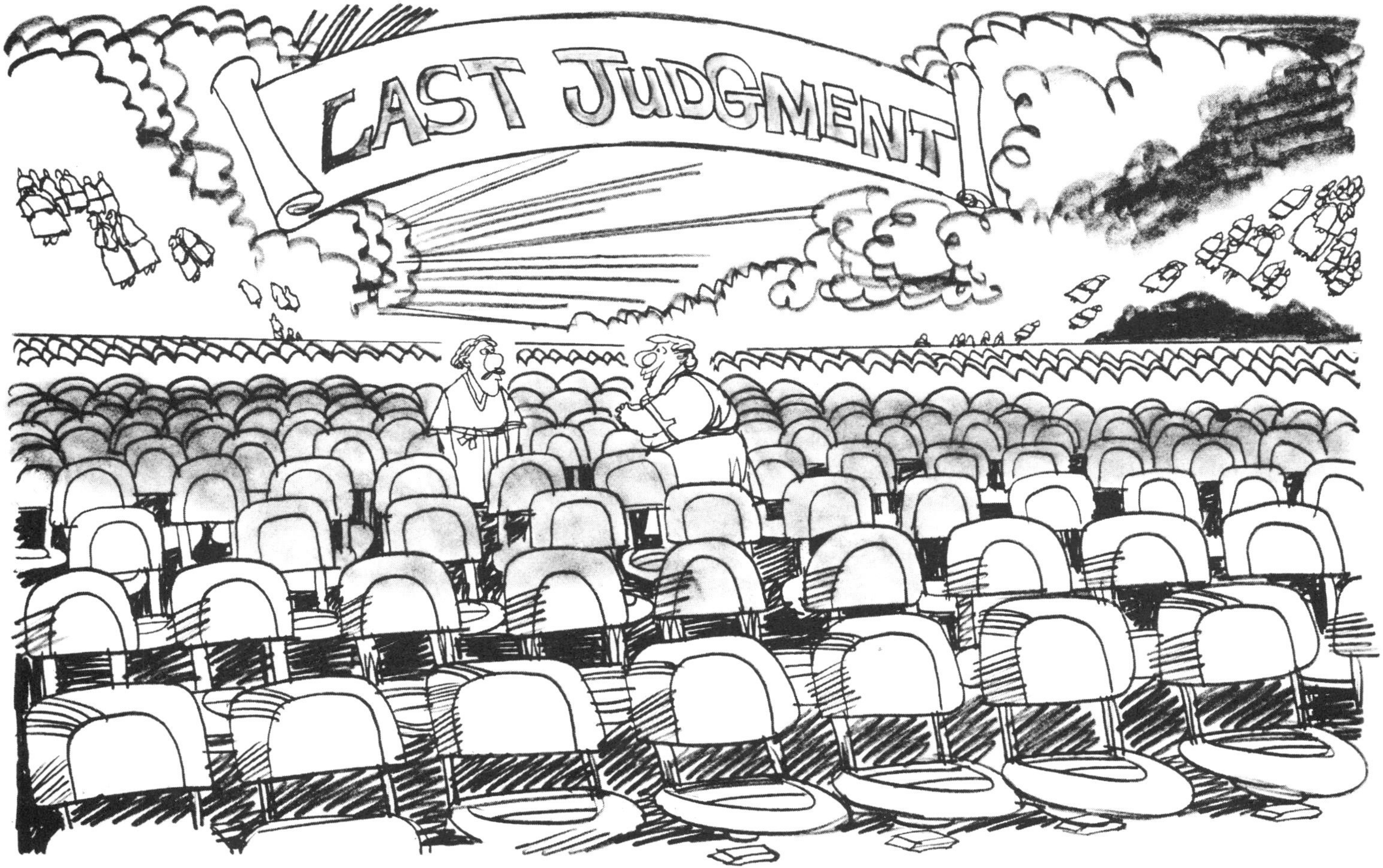
LAST JUDGMENT

"Brother, before you leave for the Telestial Kingdom, would you mind helping us take down the chairs?"

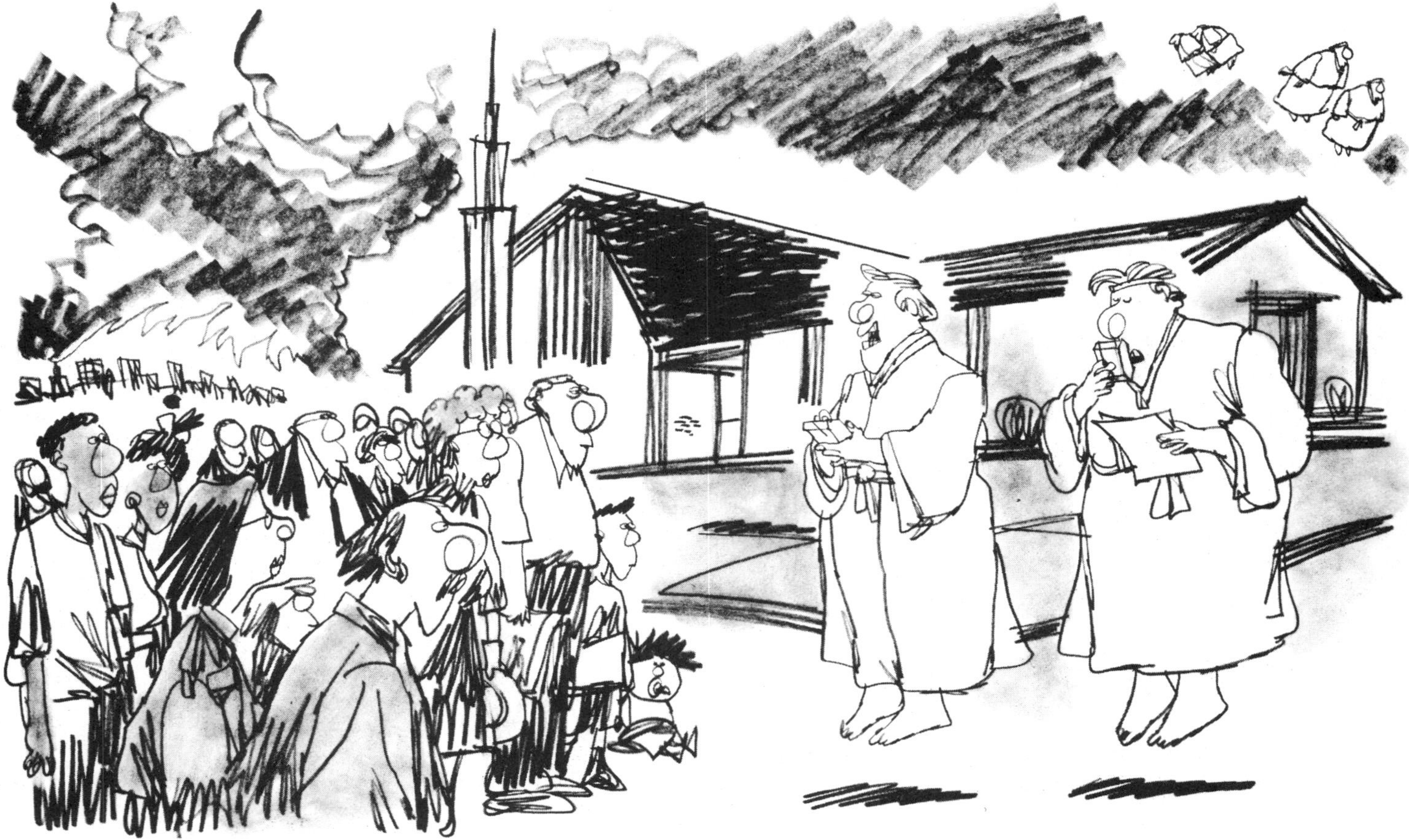

"Welcome to the Millennium. We're your assigned heavenly messengers. This will be a period of peace and harmony . . . except for those serving in the nursery."

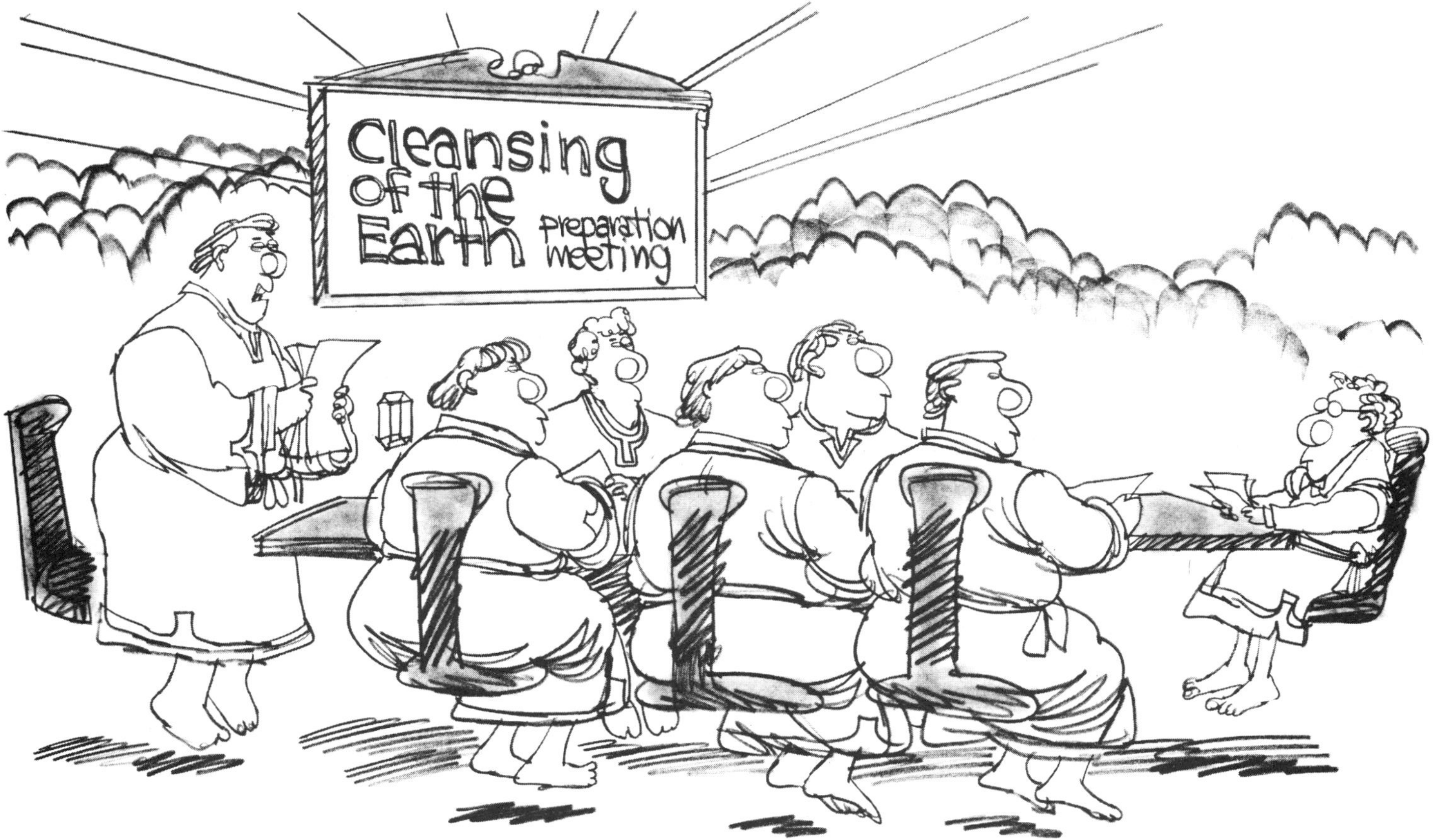
Cleansing of the Earth
preparation meeting

"Michaelson, it looks like you're once again in charge of gathering up all the aluminum ore for recycling."

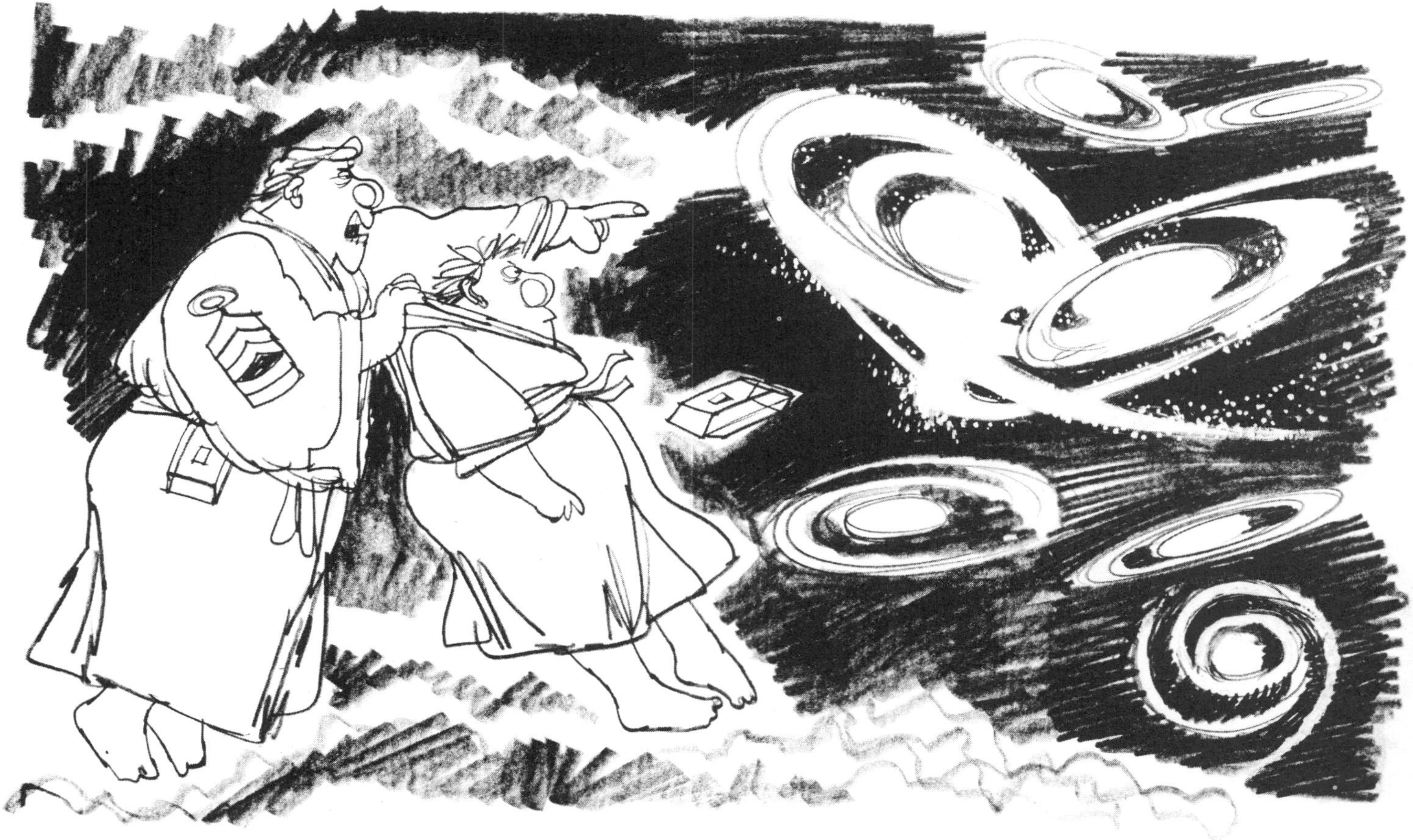

"Smithers, you idiot! You'll never be a god if you keep letting your galaxies collide!"

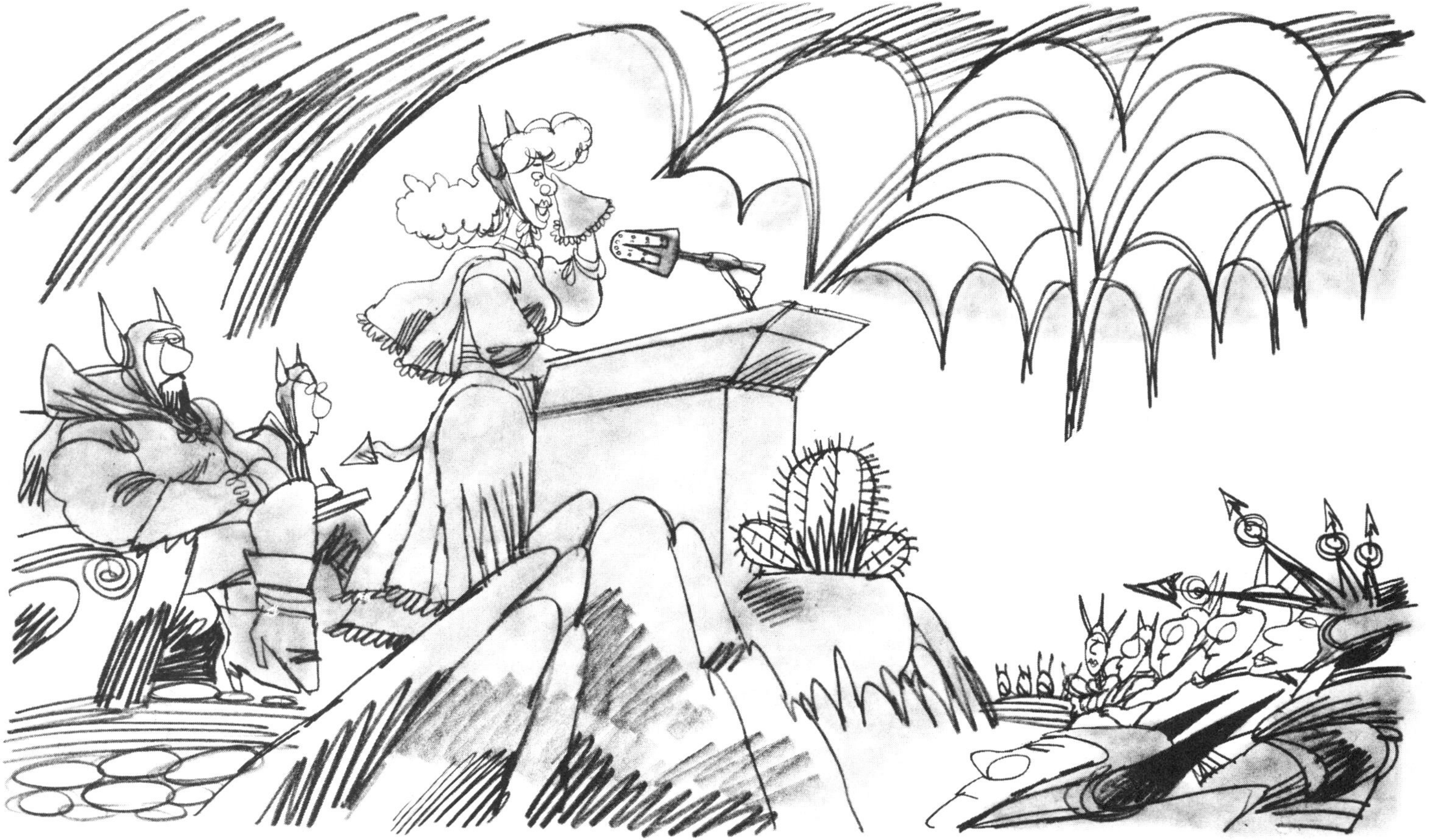

". . . I'm thankful for Lucifer and for the privilege we have of being damned together for time and all eternity . . ."

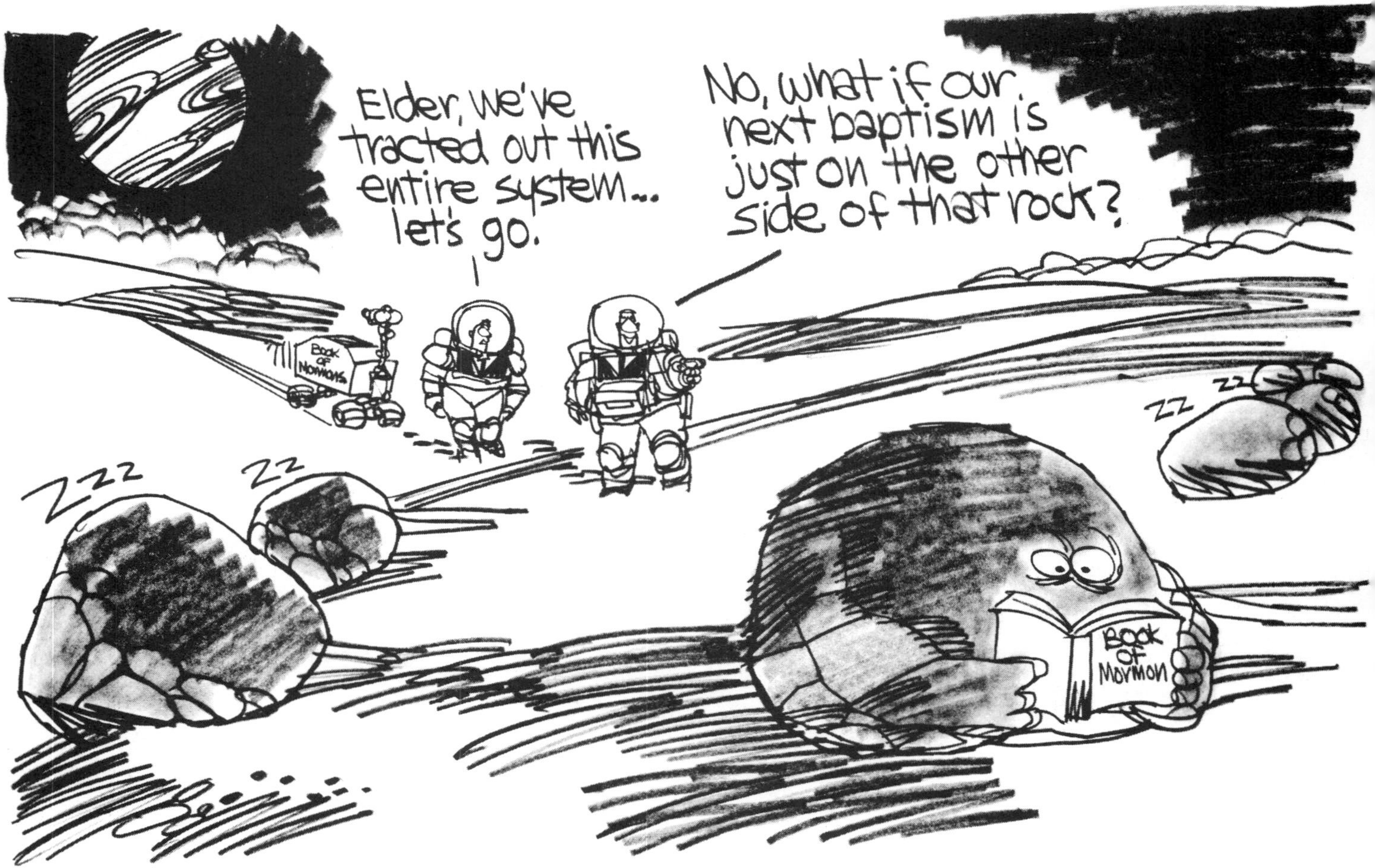
Elder, we've tracted out this entire system... let's go.
No, what if our next baptism is just on the other side of that rock?
Book of Mormons
ZZZ
ZZ
ZZ
Book of Mormon

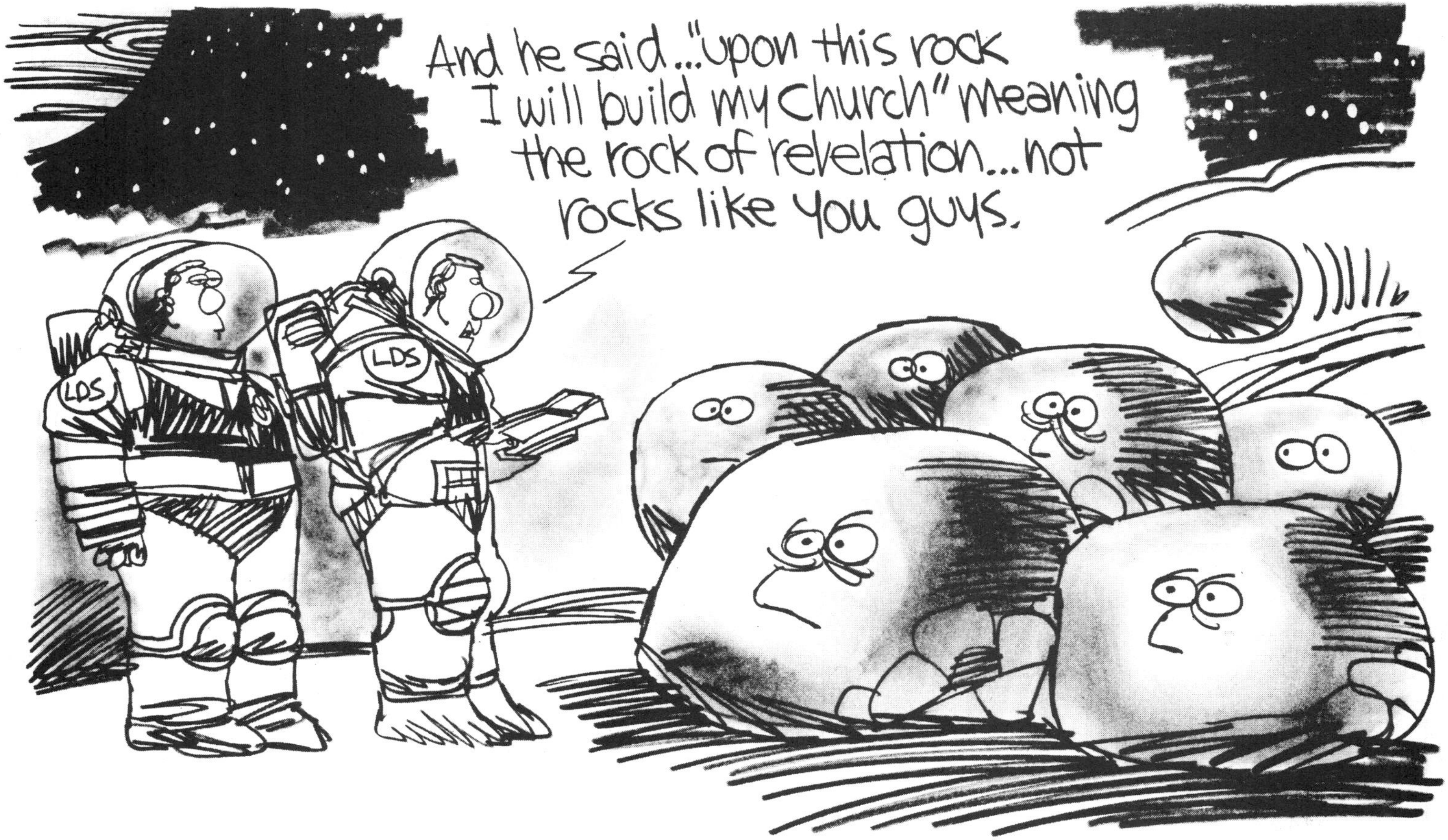
And he said..."upon this rock I will build my Church" meaning the rock of revelation...not rocks like you guys.
LDS
LDS

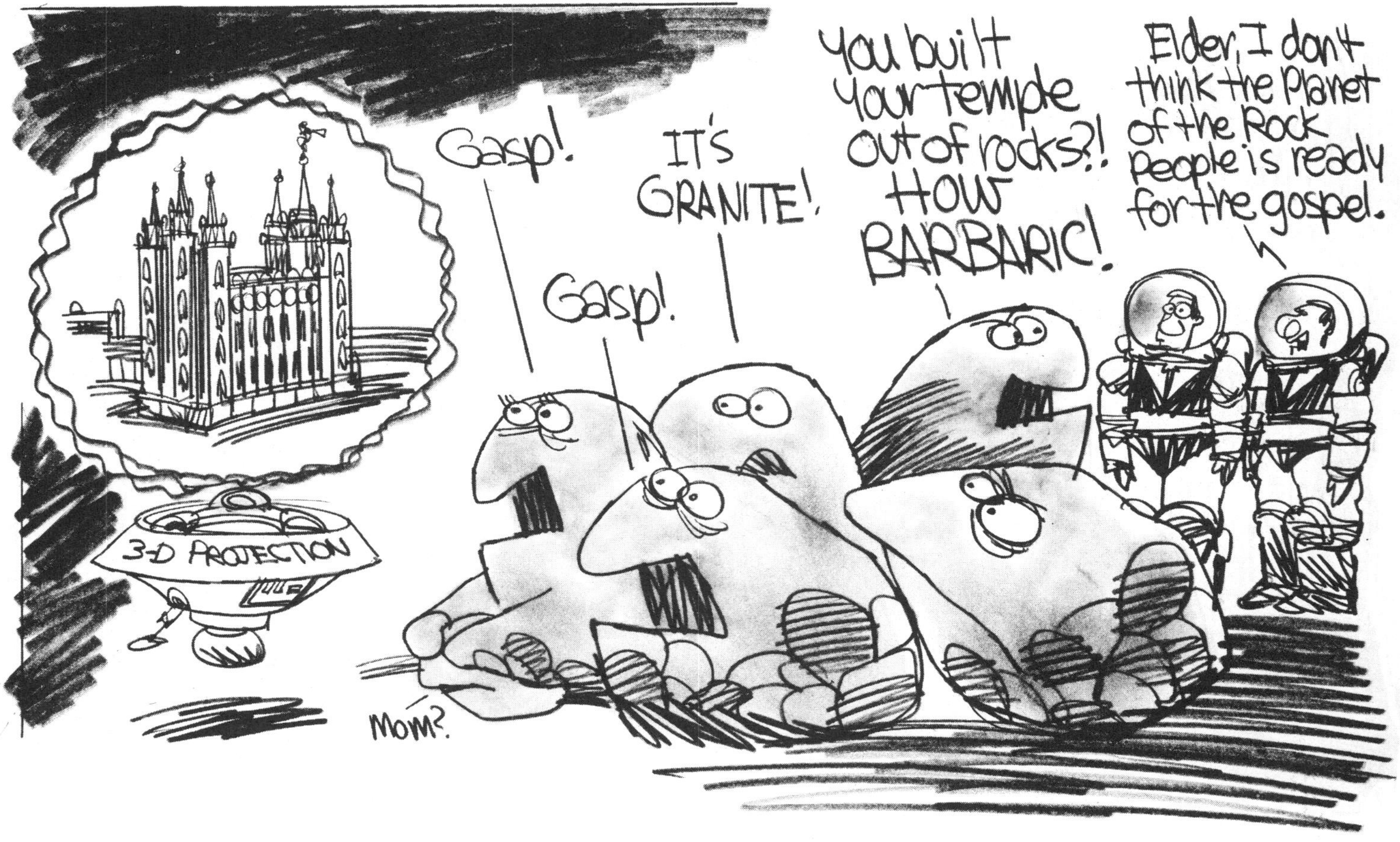
Gasp!
Gasp!
IT'S GRANITE!
You built your temple out of rocks?! HOW BARBARIC!
Elder, I don't think the Planet of the Rock People is ready for the gospel.
3-D PROJECTION
Mom?

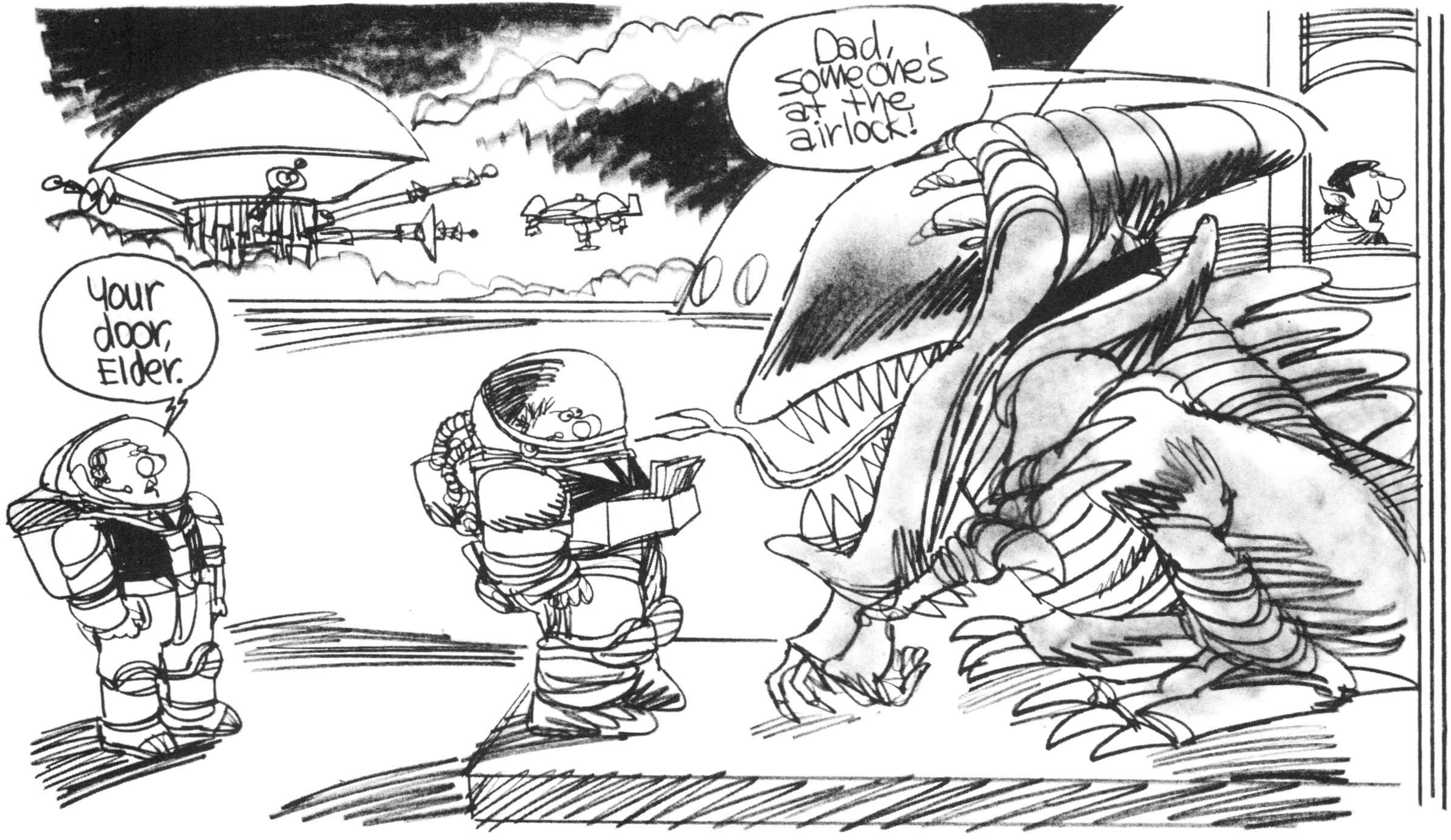
Your door, Elder.
Dad, someone's at the airlock!

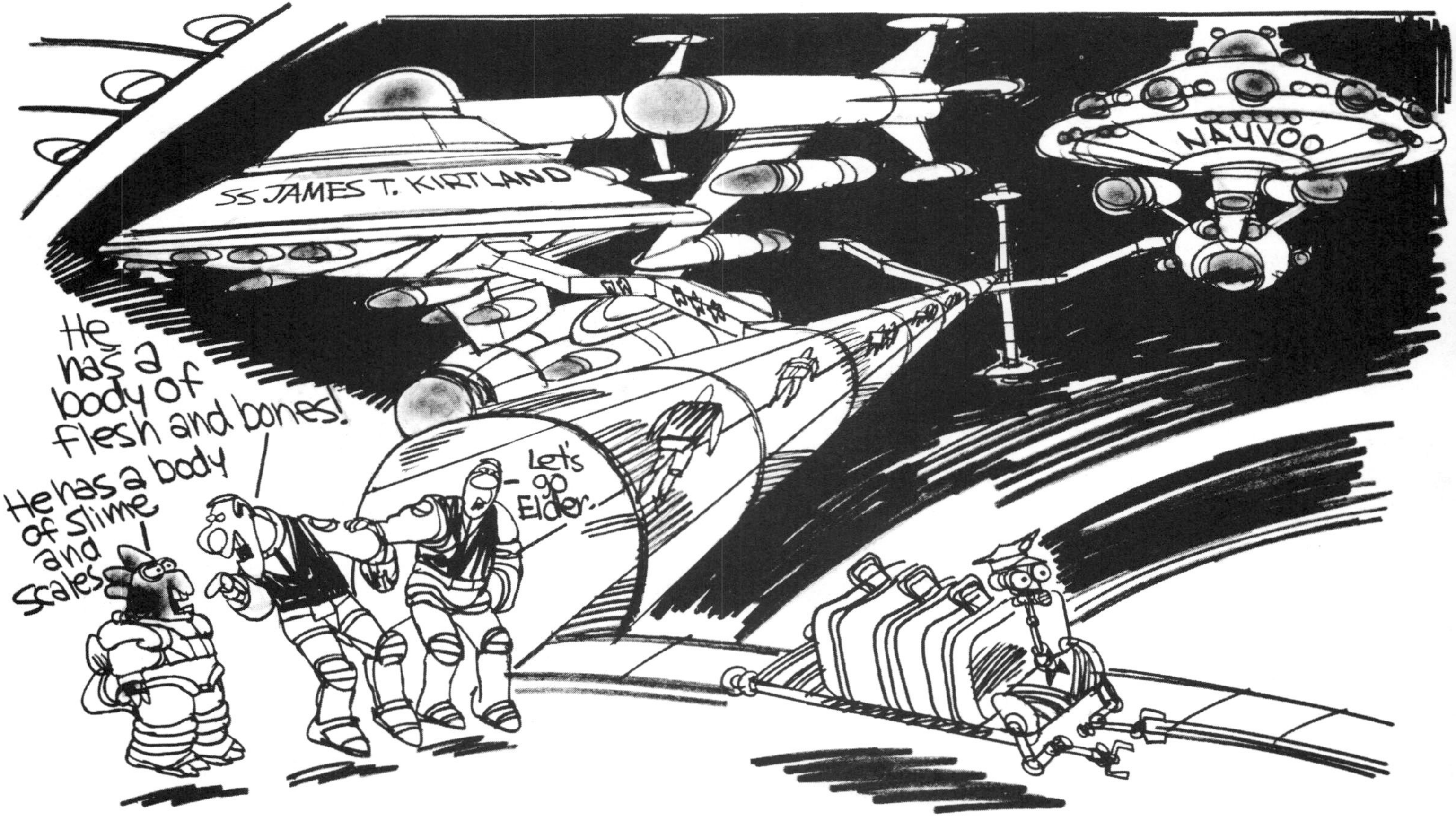
SS JAMES T. KIRTLAND
NAUVOO
He has a body of flesh and bones!
He has a body of slime and scales
Let's go Elder.

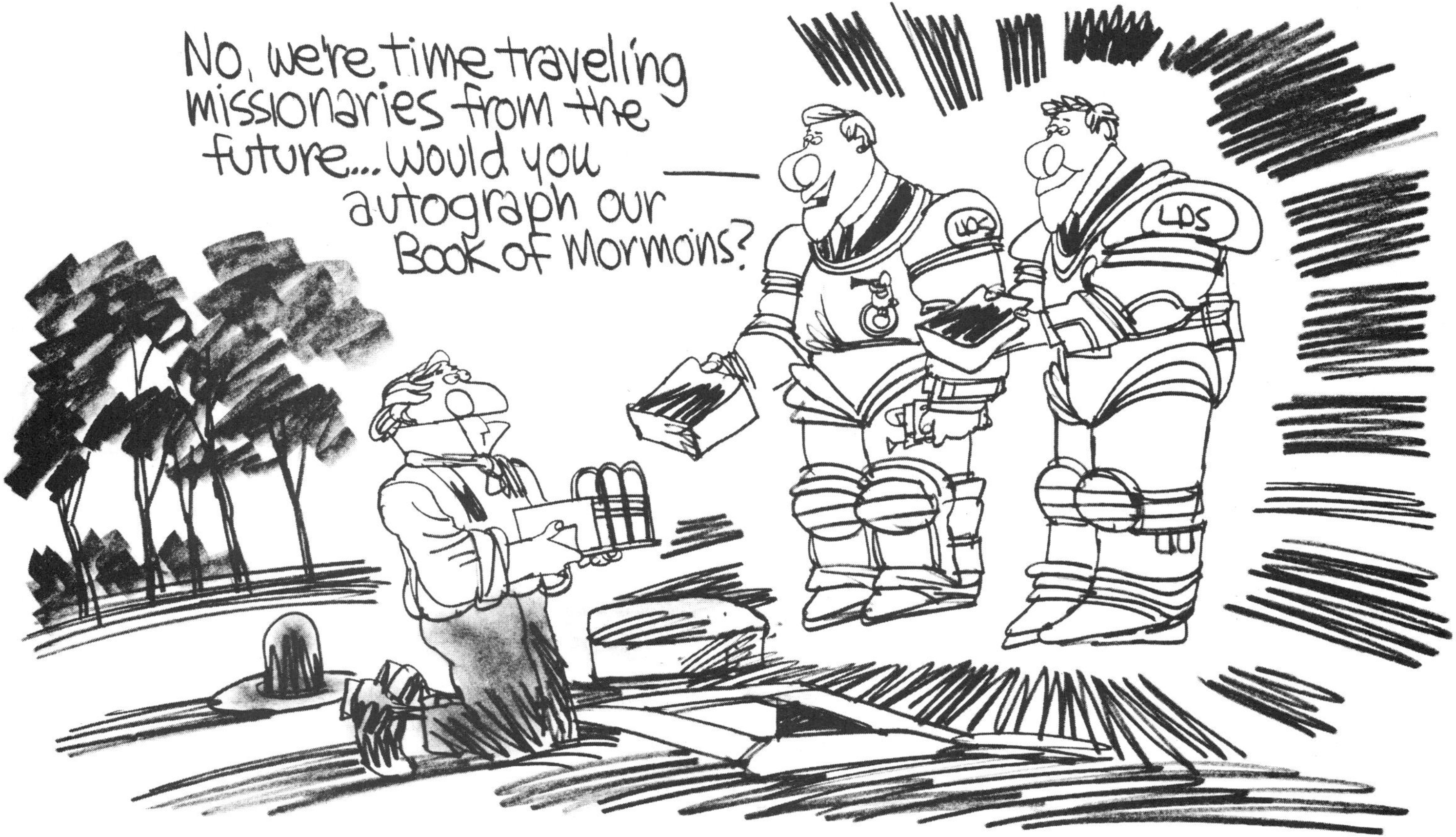
No, we're time traveling missionaries from the future.... would you autograph our Book of Mormons?
LDS
LDS

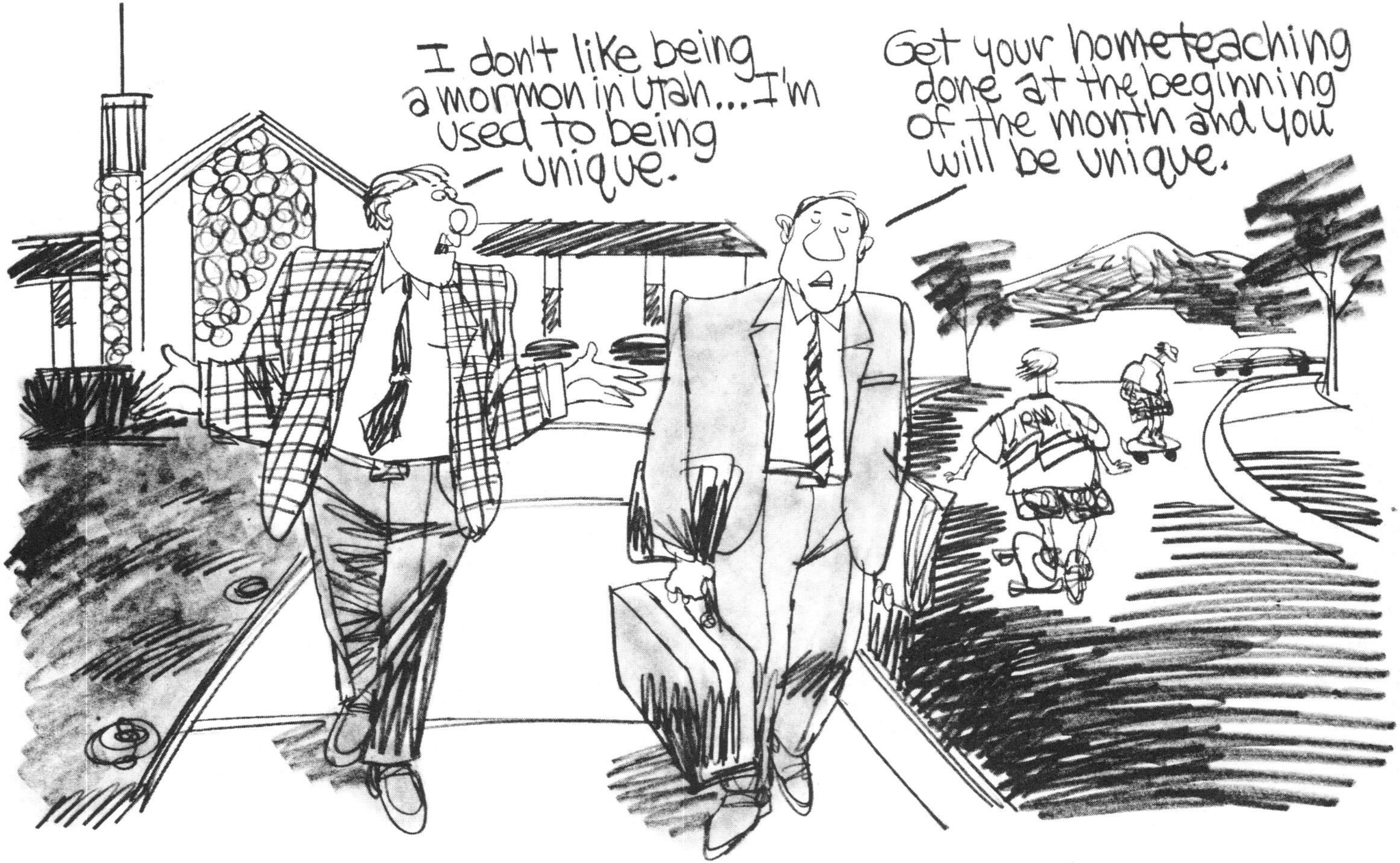
I don't like being a mormon in Utah.... I'm used to being unique.
Get your hometeaching done at the beginning of the month and you will be unique.

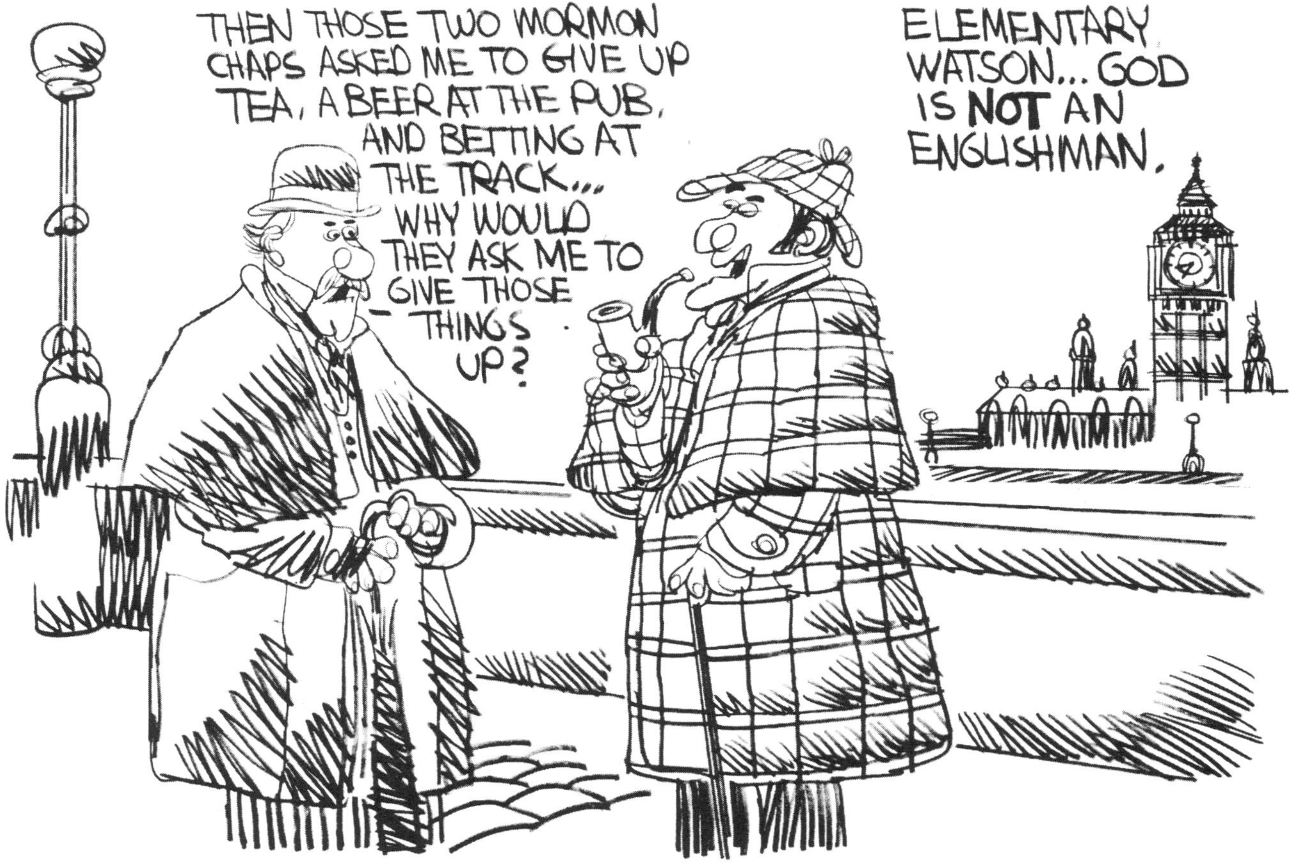
THEN THOSE TWO MORMON CHAPS ASKED ME TO GIVE UP TEA, A BEER AT THE PUB, AND BETTING AT THE TRACK.... WHY WOULD THEY ASK ME TO GIVE THOSE THINGS UP?
ELEMENTARY WATSON... GOD IS NOT AN ENGLISHMAN.

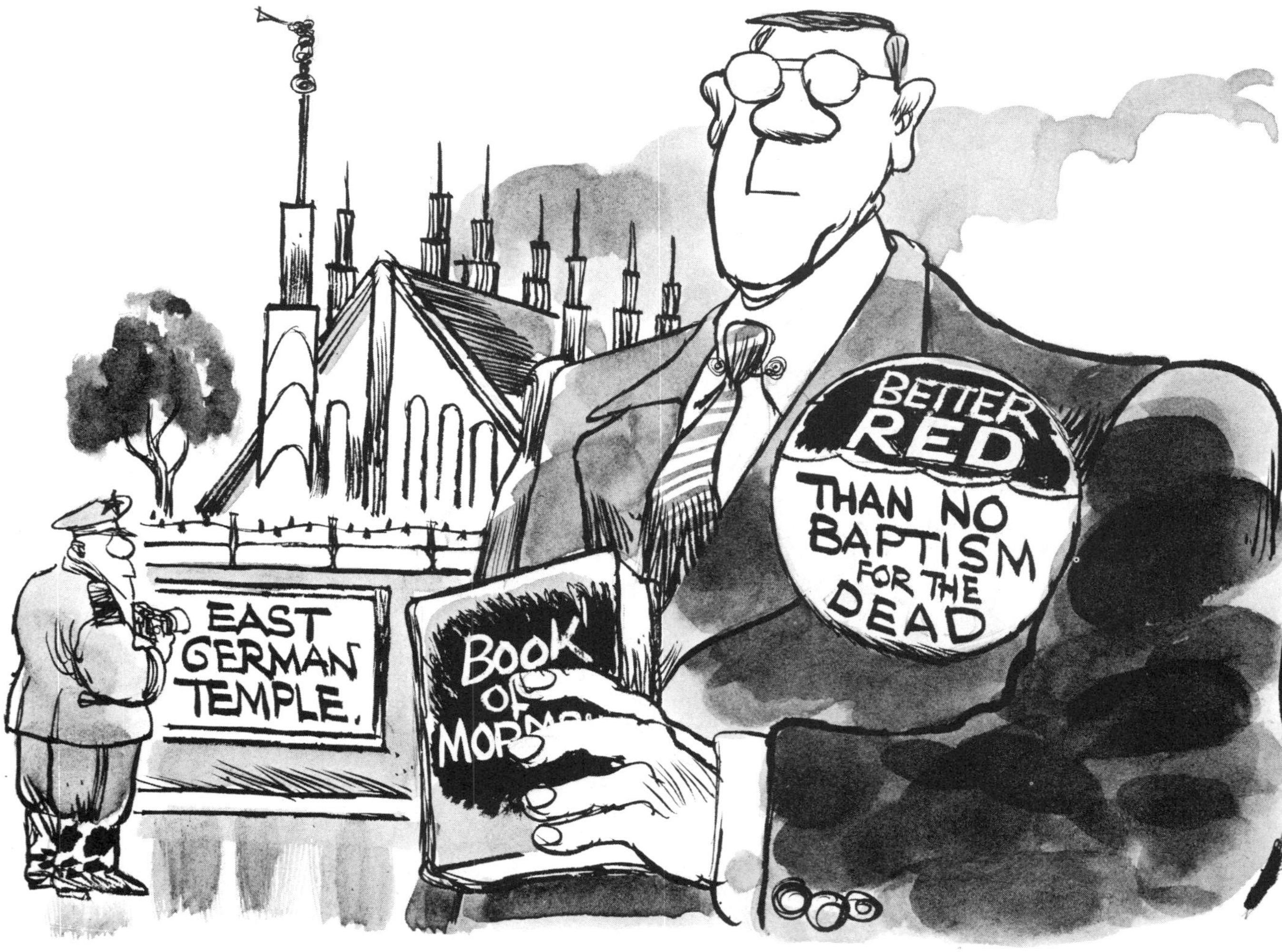
EAST GERMAN TEMPLE.
BOOK OF MORM
BETTER RED THAN NO BAPTISM FOR THE DEAD

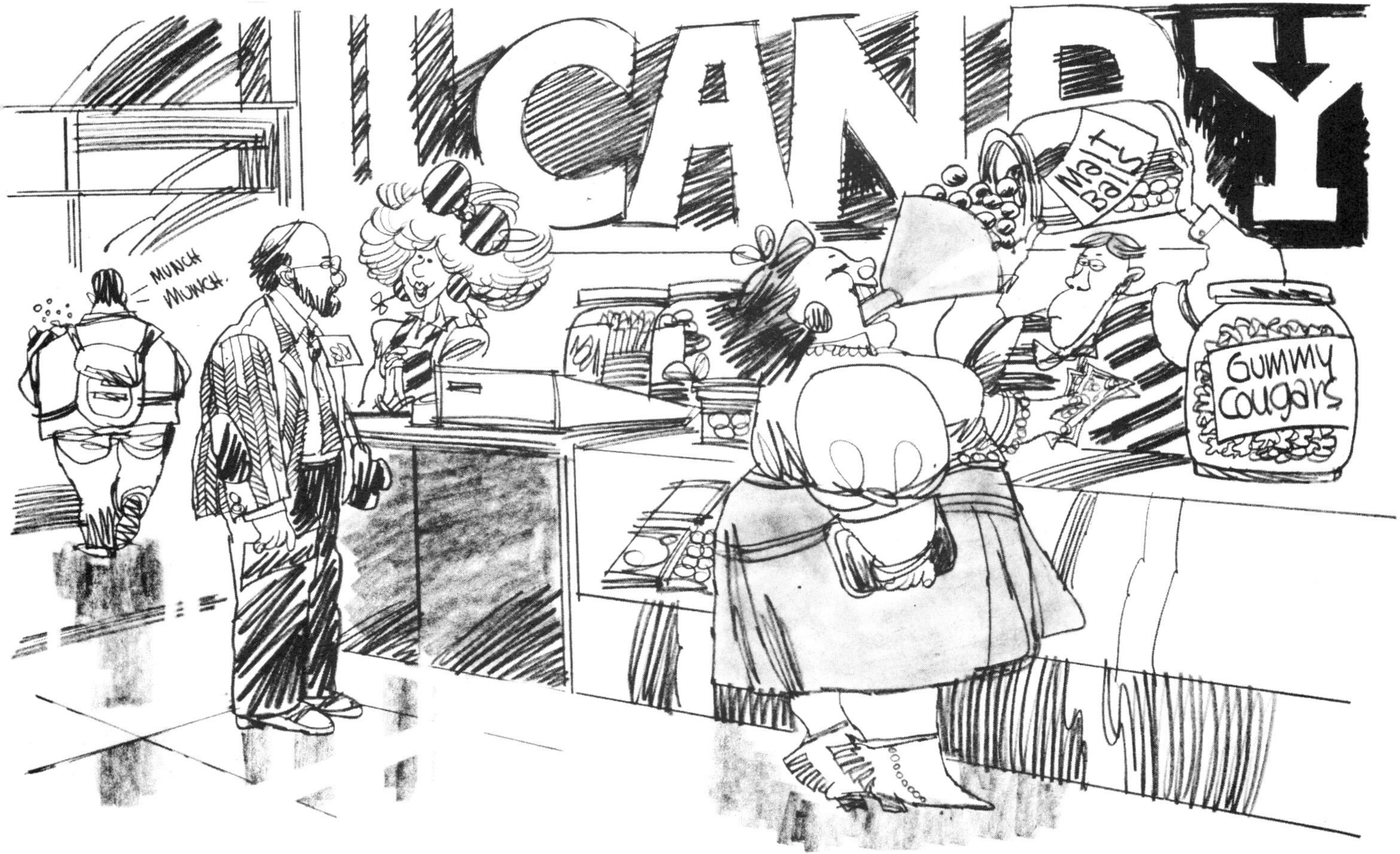
CANDY
MUNCH
MUNCH.
Malt Balls
Gummy Cougars

"I'm sorry. We don't sell caffeinated soft drinks here in the Wilkinson Center because caffeine is bad for your health."

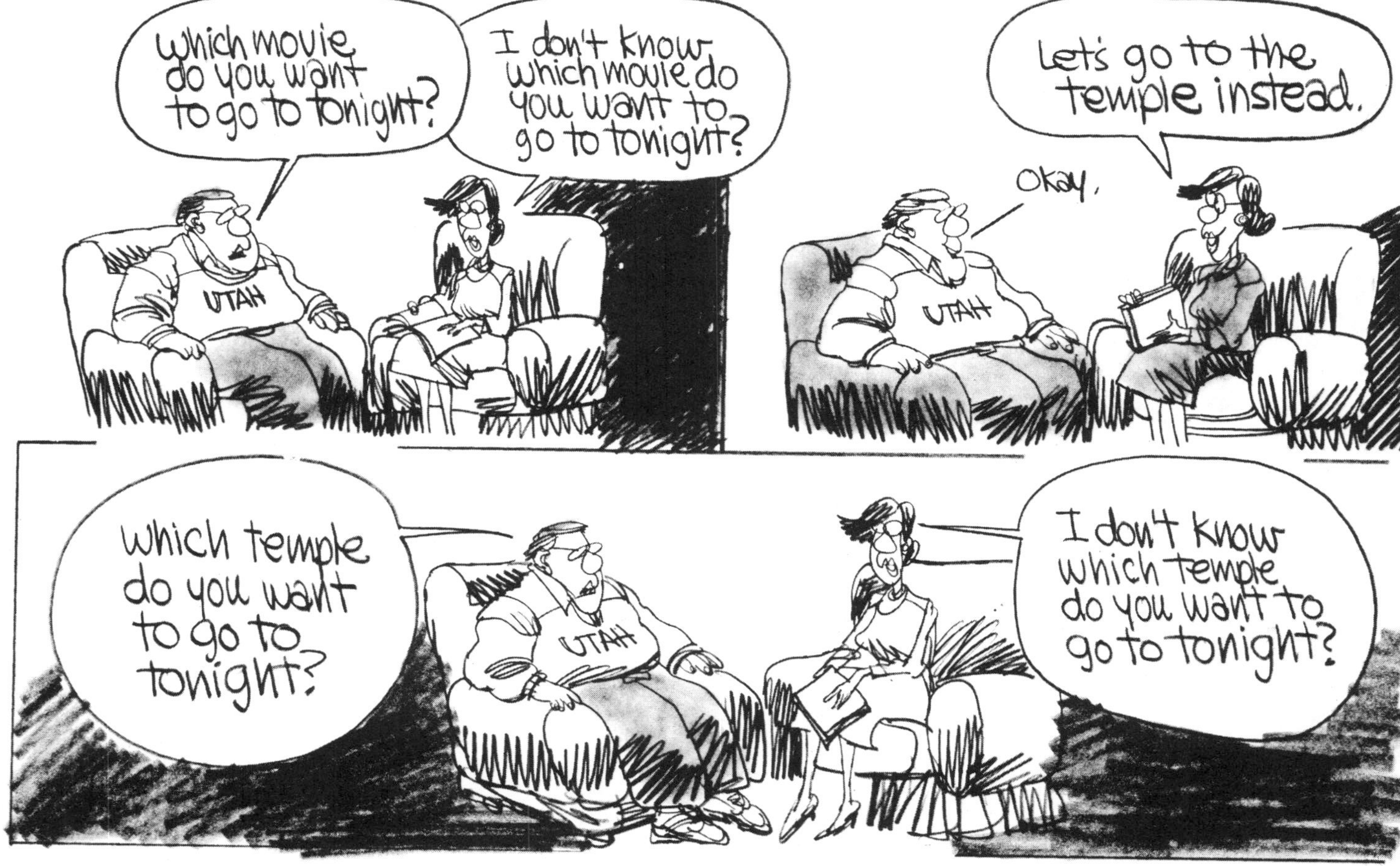
Which movie do you want to go to tonight?
I don't know which movie do you want to go to tonight?
UTAH
Let's go to the temple instead.
Okay.
UTAH
Which temple do you want to go to tonight?
UTAH
I don't know which temple do you want to go to tonight?

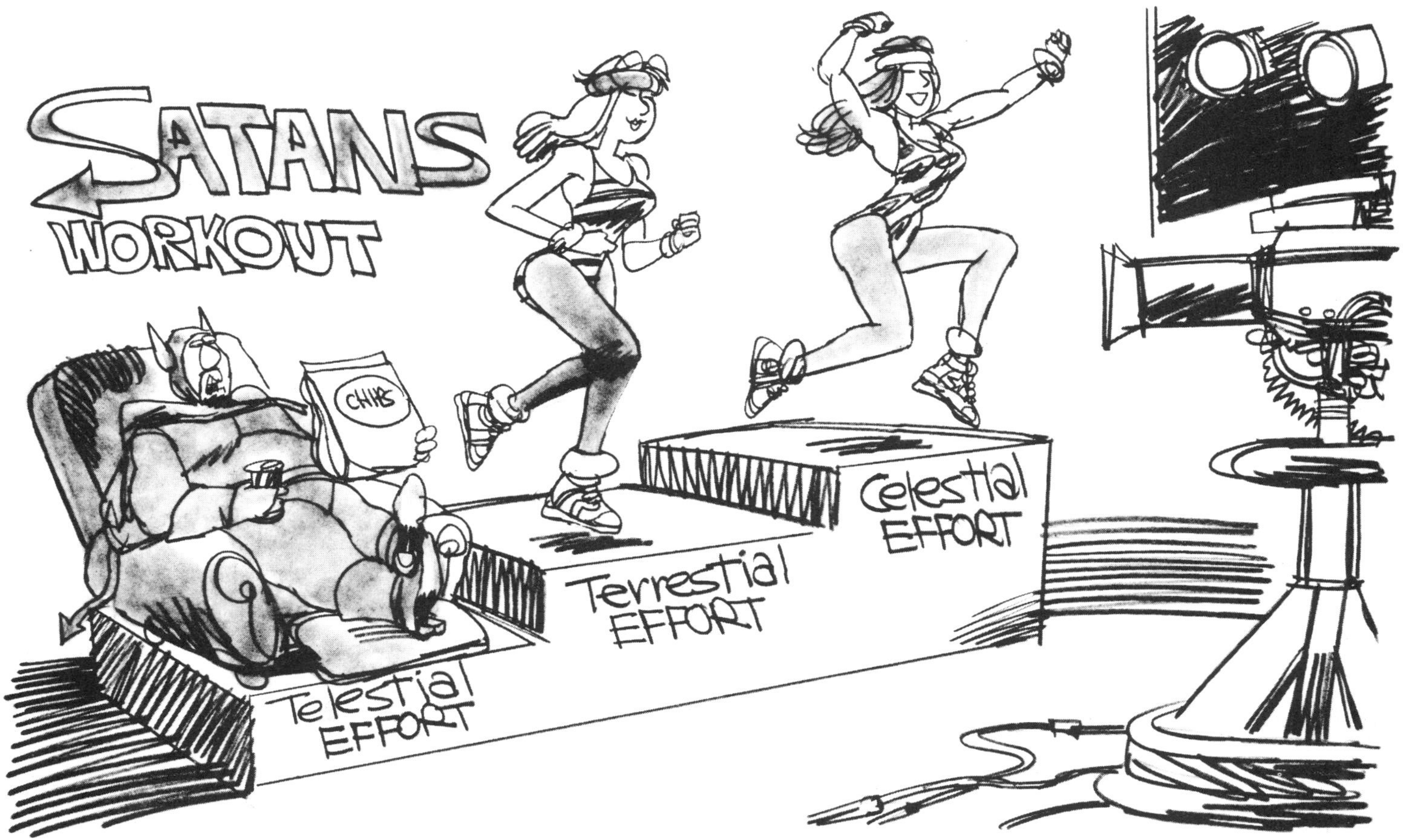
SATANS WORKOUT
CHIPS
Celestial EFFORT
Terrestial EFFORT
Telestial EFFORT

"For this next exercise all you need is a bag of potato chips."

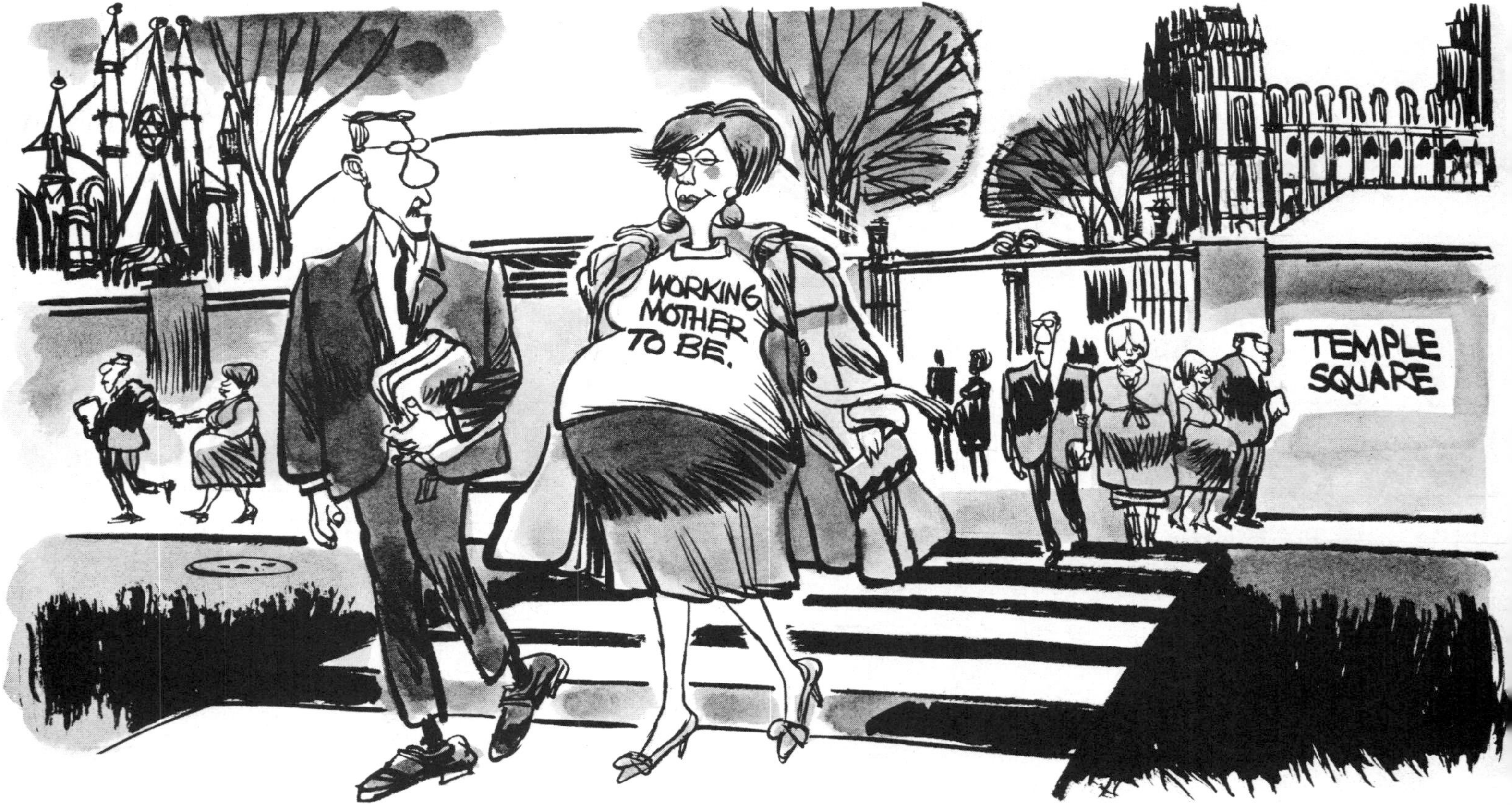
WORKING MOTHER TO BE.
TEMPLE SQUARE

"Grace, did you *have* to open your coat when the prophet came through the crowd and shook my hand?"

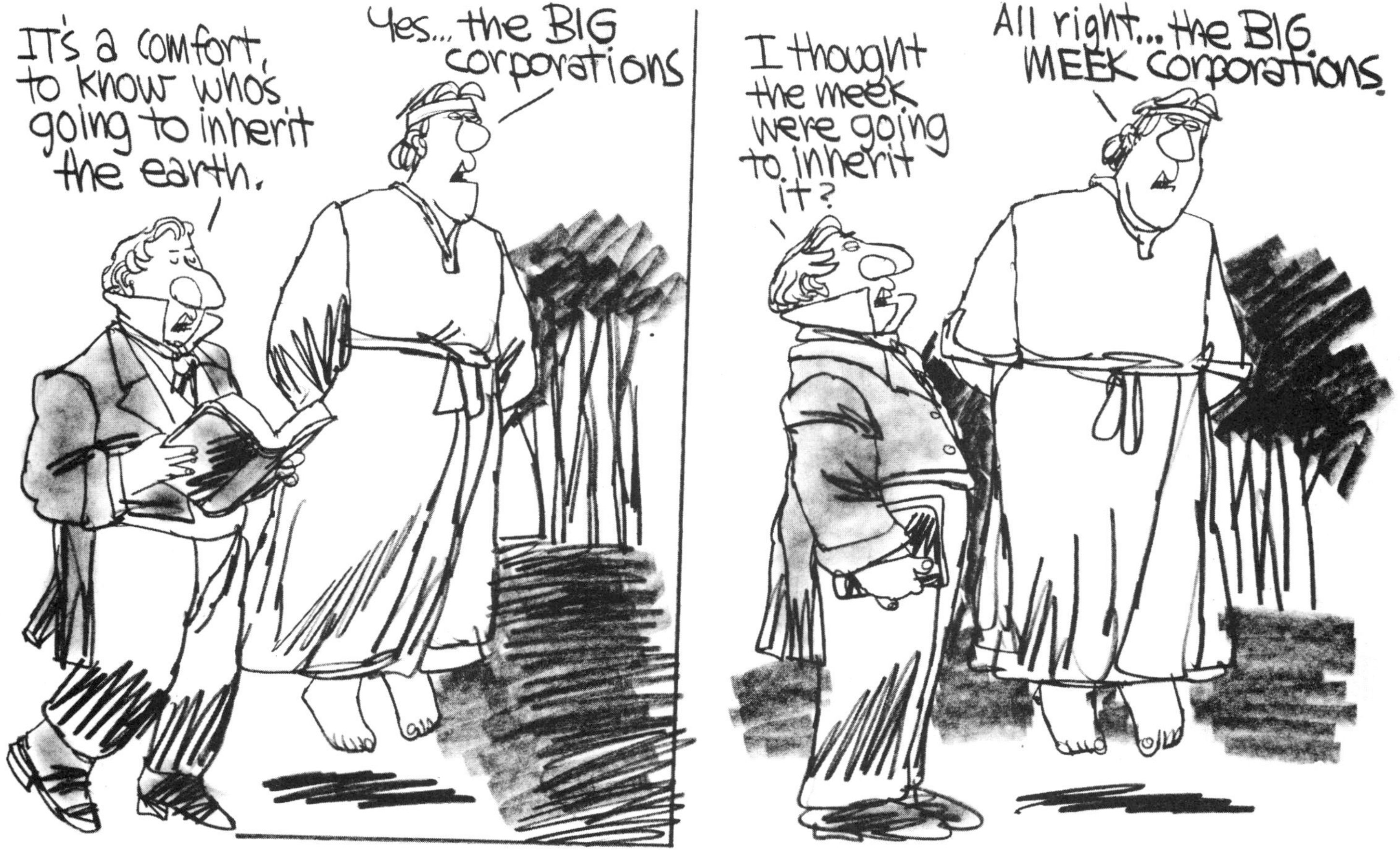
IT'S a comfort, to know who's going to inherit the earth.
Yes... the BIG corporations
I thought the meek were going to inherit it?
All right... the BIG MEEK corporations.

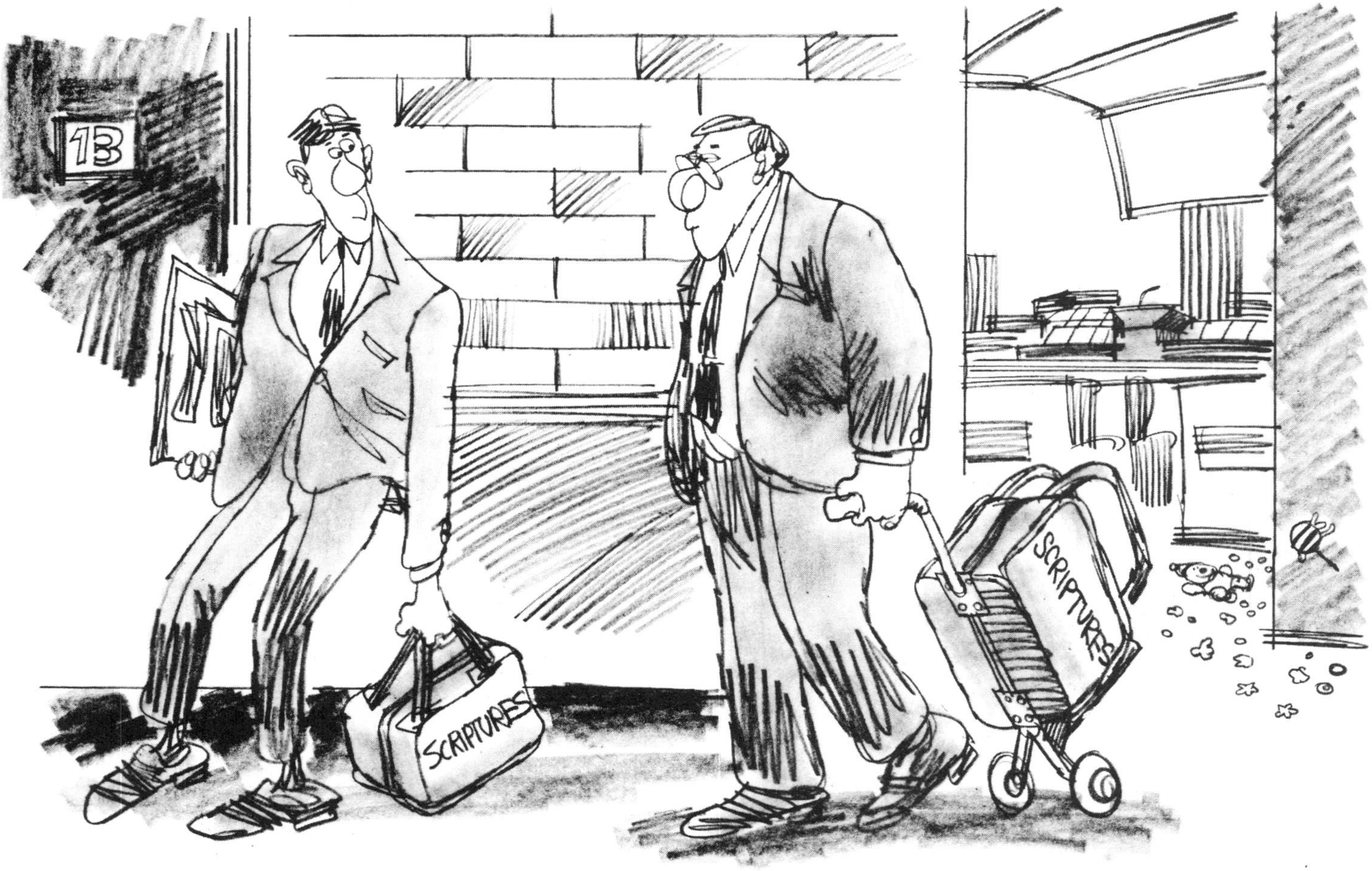
13
SCRIPTURES
SCRIPTURES